KHURAMAN ARMSTRONG

TROLLED

FROM VICTIM TO VICTOR

I0085974

WHAT OTHER READERS ARE SAYING

"I thoroughly recommend reading *Trolled* by Khuraman Armstrong. The book will take you on the emotional roller coaster ride that Khuraman and her husband had to endure at the hands of trolls.

I was shocked at what happened to her and did not think it possible. However, all the attackers' comments are clearly given, along with Khuraman's responses.

What I found fascinating and disappointing is the total lack of support that she received from the social media platforms, the police (as threats were made), and the legal system.

The journey through the minefield of trying to sort out a legal recourse is very well-written and enthralling to read.

The most outstanding part of the book is the detailed advice to readers. Based on what Khuraman learned the hard way, she explains clearly to readers how to document and deal with such troll attacks to ensure that you have all the required information to take legal action.

I firmly believe that anyone who sells and trades online should read this book to understand what can happen, and how to correctly deal with it."

—Patrick Pearl, Brisbane, Australia

"Amazing read! It resembled a Black Mirror episode. The narrative is simultaneously horrifying, depressing, and inspirational. It demonstrates how quickly and effortlessly someone's life may be completely turned upside down. Everyone is vulnerable in the digital age! I appreciate your bravery, candour, and battling spirit, Khuraman. You emerged from it stronger, more resilient, and with greater compassion in the end. And someone will have your expertise to draw on if they ever find themselves in your position (which I hope they never do!). Your narrative highlights the flaws in our society and demonstrates the necessity for legislation to be drafted and implemented. I'm proud of your wonderful book and your personality!"

—Tanya Unterberger, Melbourne, Australia

"Important story, well told. A useful guide in these digital times – what to do if someone defames you online, and how to succeed."

—Hugh Denton, Melbourne, Australia

"I want to express my fascination with his book.

I have not met the author personally, but from the moment I opened the story, I felt like I'd known her for ages. The story is so meaningful, the language is easy to read, and the overall message is very important.

I don't usually read non-fiction; I'm a hard-core fiction reader (and recently, a writer as well), but Khuraman's story touched me deeply and for multiple reasons.

First of all, I would like to say that the historical and cultural aspects of the author's heritage were described with such clarity and precision that I found myself learning and getting more interested in them.

But the main idea of the story is obviously something that none of us, at any level of publicity on social media, can be protected from. The sad reality is that the digital era brought not only great opportunities but also terrible ordeals, such as cyberbullying.

I hold the utmost respect for how the author dealt with her situation, but mostly for the fact that she took time and effort to outline her story and, most importantly, provide clear steps and directions on how to act if something like that happened to one of us. It's understood that all that is based on the author's own experience, but it doesn't make the book any less valuable."

—Katrina Zarubinski, Texas, USA

"It is heart-wrenching to realize that we are living in an era where cyberbullying can inflict immense pain and lasting damage on innocent individuals.

The power of the internet and social media platforms has provided bullies with a new avenue to target their victims, often shielded by screens and pseudonyms. They may believe that there is nothing that can be done to stop them. Wrong!

As this book has demonstrated, even in the absence of a clear jurisdictional structure to address such situations, all it takes is for an individual to stand up for what is right and be willing to go to great lengths to halt such abuse.

This book is truly eye-opening!"

—Elena Ponomareva, Sydney, Australia

"Khuraman Armstrong's *Trolled: from Victim to Victor* is a riveting account of Khuraman's courageous journey to find justice and put a halt to unprovoked and relentless attacks that threatened her livelihood, health, and peace of mind. Khuraman recounts the horrific online attacks against her as an Azerbaijani, motivated by discrimination and hatred. She provides an example of resilient and immeasurable strength that took her from 'victim to victor', teaching us a valuable lesson about taking a stand."

—Lina Hogan, Massachusetts, USA

"Such an inspiring story about fighting for justice. Sometimes when you face difficult situations in your life, where life plays unfair on you, at some point you want to give up, leave everything as it is, and forget about it, but after reading this kind of story you realise that you need to go till the end for your rights. I loved the book and the beautiful inspiring soul Khuraman has. I would like to think that what goes around comes around, and all people who hurt you will eventually get hurt as well.

Life is beautiful with beautiful people like Khuraman."

—Elvira Yafizova, Cairns, Australia

"An extremely powerful story from the strongest lady I have ever met.

Cyberbullying is the biggest online concern, and based on statistics 38% of people experience it on social media daily. The scope of cyberbullying that Khuraman Armstrong has been affected by is just giant. I highly recommend this book to anyone who wants to be aware of online cyberbullying and its consequences, and be well prepared!"

—Rana Ibrahimova, Melbourne, Australia

"This is the book by a beautiful and courageous woman who was the victim of cruel cyber bullies who organized a campaign of attacks on her online business, Enjoy Dark Chocolate. They didn't know her personally, nor had tried any of her products; they just decided to troll her, eventually destroying her small business. This book is about how she did not just give up, but fought back and won!"

—Afet Suleymanova, Virginia, USA

Published 2023, Khuraman Armstrong
Melbourne Australia
Contact: khuramanarmstrong.com

Copyright © 2023 Khuraman Armstrong

Title: *TROLLED: From Victim to Victor*
Author: Khuraman Armstrong
PRINT ISBN: 9780645872002
EBOOK ISBN: 9780645872019
Subjects: Business | Cyber Crime

Book Production: www.smartwomenpublish.com

A catalogue record for this book is available from the National Library of Australia

All rights reserved. No part of this publication may be reproduced or transmitted in any form or by any means, electronic or mechanical, including photocopying, recording, scanning or information storage and retrieval system without the prior written consent of the publisher. Every effort has been made to trace (and seek permission for use of) the primary source of material used in this book. Where the attempt has been unsuccessful, the publisher would be pleased to hear from the author/publisher to rectify any omission.

Disclaimer:

The material in this publication is of the nature of general comment only and does not represent professional advice. All material is provided for educational purposes only. We recommend to always seek the advice of a qualified professional before making any decision regarding personal and business needs. To the maximum extent permitted by law, the author and publisher disclaim all responsibility and liability to any person arising directly or indirectly from any person taking or not taking action based on the information in this publication.

CONTENTS

INTRODUCTION

Imagine you're working away one day on the exciting challenges of your growing small business when suddenly your social media notifications start pinging, seemingly every minute. Curious, you begin monitoring the activity, only to find a constant stream of vile posts, insulting comments, and negative reviews. Despite them all coming from dozens of people you don't know, and who have never been your customers, they are accusing you of being a liar and a terrorist, of poisoning people and stealing their money, and other similar atrocities, all topped off with online and phone threats of violence against you as reprisal for your supposed crimes. I am a victim of such an attack.

I am speechless! She is an open criminal person! The quality is awful! She poisons our Australian citizens with expired products which cause allergy and indigestion. People vomit after so called chocolate and finish in hospitals! Ban her illegal criminal product! She is a terrorist! She deliberately makes these chocolates to harm our beautiful Australia! 😡

Khuraman Armstrong Stay where you are and I am coming to show you the real fascist aggression, looks like you have never seen it in real life... 🙈🙉🙊 🐵

envy, yep you're right, you fuckers all envy ███████. just fuck off from the face of this earth you scum bag, stop lying, God will punish you for the lies

> doesn't recommend Khuraman Armstrong.
> 1d
>
> This company supports terrorism . You shouldn't have any deals with them.

> doesn't recommend Khuraman Armstrong.
> 8h
>
> Buyer beware, terrible customer service. No intention of resolving issues, a little rude and aggressive. Don't waste your time.

> doesn't recommend Khuraman Armstrong.
> 2d
>
> Who supports killing innocent people via their business and trying to sell chocolates. If you support this business you support terrorism. Such a sick individual.

While I was tempted to call out my attackers by name in this book, I have made the conscious decision not to do so as I refuse to give them any recognition or notoriety for their hateful actions. However, although they remain nameless, their actions serve as a powerful reminder of the importance of this fight.

If you think these examples are alarming, brace yourself for the chapter titled **The Mob Attack**. In that section, I recount the terrifying experience of being targeted by fifty strangers who launched this smear campaign against me. Even more frightening was receiving a series of phone calls from aggressive, anonymous individuals issuing death threats against me, including the gruesome prospect of beheading me. I have never known fear like it.

As you may already know, the internet has become a breeding ground for disinformation, bullying and trolling, and it has reached epidemic proportions. With billions of users on social media platforms, people have unrestricted access to express their opinions, regardless of how hurtful they may be to others.

While the media often focuses on large-scale disinformation campaigns associated with politics or war, the majority of online hurt is caused by mean-spirited offenders, either individuals or groups, who engage in bullying, trolling or defamation of others, as was my experience. And despite the alarming statistics regularly published by the authorities highlighting the frequency of online trolling and abuse, as I reference more directly in the sub-chapter titled **Sadly, I am not alone** and in **Appendix III** at the end of the book, the human toll of online bullying and defamation is often overlooked, making it easy for people to think "it could never happen to me". But it can happen to anyone, just as it happened to me. And that was only the start of the ordeal.

In the chapter titled **The Help That Never Came**, I recount my frustration with the police, regulatory bodies and Facebook's lacklustre response to my attackers, and my realisation of what a relatively lawless environment the online space remains today.

That said, in the chapter **My Legal Journey**, I share how I pursued some of my offenders through the justice system, ultimately securing judgement in my favour and gaining some financial settlements. However, the compensation I have received pales in comparison to the legal costs I have incurred, and the two and a half years of stress I have endured.

So why did I choose to take legal action? With no other avenues of intervention available, I was faced with the horrible choice of either letting the offenders go unpunished, or taking a stand to hold them accountable and to send a message that 'enough is enough'.

Through my own experience, I also realised how scarce meaningful guidance was for victims of online attacks. Thus, I decided to write this book and share four key insights to help others navigate similar situations:

1. How easily such attacks can happen to any of us, at any time, over which we have so little control, thus the urgent need for more decisive intervention from social media platforms and governing bodies.
2. My own emotional and financial battle through our justice system to restore my reputation and hold my attackers accountable. After reading the chapter **My Legal Journey**, you will understand why you should only consider suing for defamation as a last resort, regardless of what you may think are the merits of your case, and only after seeking reputable legal advice.
3. The steps you should take to protect your interests and legal outcomes if you or someone you love ever experiences online trolling or defamation. Be sure to bookmark Appendix I titled **The First Twenty-Four Hours** as it provides a step-by-step guide on what to do during the crucial, emotionally charged first hours of such an attack. This chapter also explains how to secure evidence you will need if you decide to engage the authorities or justice system to deal with the offenders.
4. How it's possible to fight back from such an experience and regain a positive, trusting and creative outlook on life, by moving from a victim to a creator state.

In writing this book, it is not my aim to portray myself as a victim. While I was indeed targeted in the attack, my focus is on resilience, and using my experience to empower and support others. Moreover, I believe that we can all make a positive impact by standing up against online harassment, and advocating for a safer, more respectful digital world.

This process has also helped me in my own journey of healing and recovery. Despite some of the challenging content and themes, I sincerely hope that you will find this book informative, useful, and even enjoyable.

1. ABOUT ME

Whilst this book isn't about my life story, for context I need to explain a little about my background and myself.

MY AZERBAIJANI STORY

This story begins in my homeland of Azerbaijan, a land steeped in history and culture, and where 'East meets West'. Azerbaijan is known as the Land of Fire, and for good reason. Fire has been a part of our lives for centuries, providing us with light, warmth and safety. This reverence for fire is ingrained in my DNA, and it fuels a passion that burns inside me for everything I do. As I take you through this story, you will see how this passion has driven me to confront, and overcome, some significant challenges.

Growing up in the Soviet Union, my childhood was anything but dull. My parents were both adventurous spirits, eager to explore all the corners of the vast Union of Soviet Socialist Republics (USSR). As my father was a doctor and my mother an engineer, they had the means and the curiosity to take me and my two brothers on road trips to many different republics, where we were exposed to a wealth of cultures, traditions and foods. From the snow-capped peaks of the Caucasus to the sandy shores of the Black Sea, we saw it all. Each trip was a new adventure, and I was always eager to see what lay ahead. These experiences left an indelible mark on me, shaping my worldview and instilling a love of travel and discovery that has stayed with me to this day.

As a child, I was drawn to the culinary arts, and it was my mother who first instilled in me a love for cooking. Growing up in our culture, where food and gatherings go hand in hand, meant that every celebration revolved around delicious meals and lively dancing. I was always eager to lend a hand in the kitchen and join in on the socialising.

Every summer, we would travel to Kalbajar, my father's birthplace, to spend time with his relatives. It was there that my grandmother and namesake, Khuraman, was born. In fact, my name itself carries a special meaning: elegant, graceful. Unfortunately, in Australia, where I now reside, my name can be a tongue twister for most locals, so I often go by Kay, a shortened and anglicised version of my name, although ironically, the K in Khuraman is silent.

One of my fondest childhood memories is of travelling with my father through the remote mountain communities and small villages of Azerbaijan, which were always filled with wonder and excitement. My dad's love for Azerbaijani carpets was contagious, and it wasn't long before I found myself utterly captivated by the artform. I'll never forget the first time I witnessed carpet weavers at work. Their pride and passion for their craft was palpable, and it touched my heart in a way I hadn't thought possible. From that moment on, Azerbaijani carpets, particularly those from the Quba-Shirvan and Karabakh regions, have held a special place in my heart.

For me, Azerbaijani carpets are more than just floor coverings. They're a powerful, sublime and unique form of storytelling. Each element on a carpet tells a story, and every symbol has a meaning. Tragedies, love stories and traditions are all woven into the intricate patterns, making these rugs true testaments to history.

So when I graduated from the State University of Culture and Arts with a bachelor's degree in the management of cultural/educational institutions, I was beyond excited to secure a job as a curator at the world-renowned Azerbaijan National Carpet Museum. Being able to see these magnificent works of art every day—to touch them, to study them and the stories behind them, and to imagine the people who wove them—was a dream come true. The museum's oldest and most treasured exhibit, the 17th-century carpet Ajdahali ('Dragon') from the Karabakh region of Azerbaijan, was a particular favourite of mine.

If you have the opportunity to visit Baku in Azerbaijan, be sure not to miss the remarkable and one-of-a-kind National Carpet Museum, pictured below; the building itself boasts a unique and striking architecture.

However, these carpets also brought me a sharp realisation of the senselessness of war. As I explain later in this book, the Karabakh region of Azerbaijan has been illegally occupied since 1993. During the more than thirty years of occupation, the region has lost countless private carpet collections, including that of my father's friend, the History-Ethnography Museum.

As someone who was working in the museum at the time, and who is deeply passionate about Azerbaijani carpets and their history, it was heartbreaking for me to see these priceless works of art being stolen or destroyed. Fortunately, we were able to save around six hundred carpets from Shusha city, thanks to the heroic efforts of the museum director, who acted just before the occupation. These carpets are now on display in an exhibition titled Burned Culture, reminding everyone of the power and importance of preserving our cultural heritage.

As I entered my thirties, I felt a strong desire to explore more of the world, which led me to Australia, where I have resided since 2005.

MY AUSTRALIAN STORY

My current surname, Armstrong, reflects my marriage and new Australian home. Coincidentally, Armstrong is of Scottish heritage and carries the motto, "Invictus Maneo" ("I remain unvanquished"), which is remarkably prophetic, as you will read.

After finishing my studies in accounting, I lived in Brisbane and worked as an investigation and assessment officer for the government.

My passion for an active and healthy lifestyle has led me to regularly hit the gym and learn Latin dancing. Seeking a more diverse community, I moved to Melbourne in 2013 and have enjoyed the city's multicultural atmosphere ever since.

Growing up in a family that values diversity and cultural exploration, I have always been fascinated by the beauty and richness of different cultures around the world. Despite the vast physical and cultural distance between Azerbaijan and Australia, I have found many similarities between the two countries, particularly their shared values of multiculturalism and acceptance. As a firm believer in the power of diversity to foster innovation and growth, I have made it my life's mission to celebrate and promote different cultures and cuisines. Through my blog, and collaborations with other cultural enthusiasts, I showcase the vibrant diversity of global cuisine and cultural events, and I hope to inspire others to embrace multiculturalism and recognise the unique contributions that each culture brings to our society.

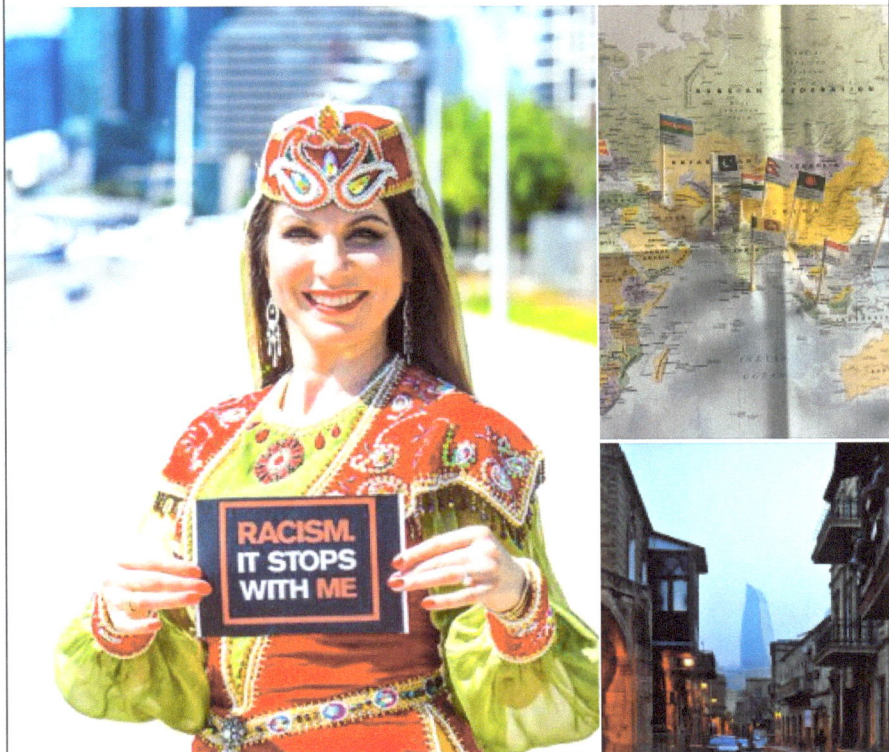

Khuraman Armstrong
April 1, 2017

Super excited. Our management at work was very impressed with my effort that I put towards Harmony Day (Multicultural Day). I wore my traditional costume and also participated in UN Day for elimination of racism, I spoke about cultural diversity in Azerbaijan. Everyone was interested in history of my country and , of course, the food that I shared.

I have also prepared the map with flag of different countries to show how diverse was our team.From 18 people in our team we have representatives of 14 countries, the best multicultural environment I have ever worked in.

And now our management has decided to kick-start a monthly multicultural write up based on a staff member so everyone can learn more about their culture. They have decided to start with me.

So I spending my Saturday night writing up a story about my country. Икмет Садыхов I am going to use some photos of Baku taken by you:)

Facebook post from 2017
celebrating Multiculturalism

Despite having obtained two degrees, I have a continuous thirst for new knowledge and personal growth. I actively seek out self-development courses and insights that can help me improve my life. As a natural networker, I enjoy conversing with people to learn about their interests and dislikes. This has made adapting to the Australian culture and learning a new language relatively easy for me.

During my time in Brisbane, I was introduced to the exciting world of internet marketing and entrepreneurship, which really inspired and motivated me. Through various courses, I enhanced my skills and learned to set big goals and dream big. One of my most significant aspirations was to become self-employed and have the freedom to live life on my own terms, and I continue to invest in self-development to realise and maintain this ambition.

I'm also fortunate that my husband Graeme is a fellow entrepreneur, who is very encouraging and supportive of my business and social endeavours. His experience as a successful business executive has also been invaluable during my legal battle, and I can't thank him enough for his unwavering support and professional contribution.

MY ONLINE BUSINESSES

Since 2014, I have dedicated my life to becoming a self-made entrepreneur and developing my online brand. As a result, I have an established online brand and presence, with several active ventures:
- First up is Enjoy Dark Chocolate, my chocolate business, because let's face it, who doesn't enjoy dark chocolate?
- Next, we have AgelessYou, a beauty and wellbeing brand partnership that helps people to look and feel their best in no time.
- Moving on to KhuramanArmstrong.com, my one-stop-shop website for all luxury gifting and lifestyle needs.
- Then Cooking and Culture, where I contribute to the community by sharing my cooking recipes and health tips.
- And finally, Global Storytellers, a Meetup group.

Most of my business prospecting and transactions are conducted online, particularly, yet not exclusively, within the Russian-speaking community, using the following website and Facebook pages:

- https://www.KhuramanArmstrong.com (my central website)
- https://www.facebook.com/Kay.Abdullayeva (my personal profile page)
- https://www.facebook.com/KhuramanArmstrong (a business page about all my businesses and services)
- https://www.facebook.com/EnjoyDarkChocolate (a business page dedicated to my chocolate business)

For full contact details, see page 115.

I have loved the taste of dark chocolate all my life, and I developed an awareness of its health benefits long ago. As part of an online marketing course, I purchased the Enjoy Dark Chocolate URL and started my Enjoy Dark Chocolate Facebook group to blog about dark chocolate and its health benefits.

Shortly after moving to Melbourne in 2013, I was invited to join the 7,500-member Facebook group, Russian Women's Network, for Russian-speaking women living in the city. With my interest in health and nutrition, I soon became an active contributor to this group by constantly sharing my cooking recipes and health tips. I was an active sponsor of many fundraisers and events organised by this group.

My passion and dedication to my business, Enjoy Dark Chocolate, is what I am most known for. It all started in 2015 when, after creating an experimental range of dried fruits dipped in dark chocolate, I shared the range with family and close friends. The positive feedback and encouragement I received prompted me to take a hesitant step towards becoming an online chocolate retailer, and Enjoy Dark Chocolate was born.

Since then, I have worked tirelessly with my team of artisan chocolatiers to create individually crafted and exquisite chocolate delights that contain only the freshest and highest-quality berries, fruits, nuts and dairy products, all enrobed in the world's finest organic dark chocolate.

My chocolates not only taste decadent and irresistible, but also provide real health benefits through their natural, organic, and high-antioxidant ingredients, without any preservatives or artificial colours or flavours. From the beginning it was important to me that they were kosher and halal compliant so they could be offered to the wider Australian community.

Starting Enjoy Dark Chocolate on my own, without any funds or support, was challenging. In 2016, I sold my apartment in Brisbane to fund my business and support myself financially as my salary was not enough to provide additional investment in my business. I have always approached my chocolate business as a fully professional operation, leaving full-time corporate employment in 2017 to work full-time on the business. Despite the risks, I was committed to making the business a success.

Building the business from scratch was not easy. I had to establish a team of employees and build great relationships with suppliers. Since I have never been a chocolatier myself, I relied on professional chocolatiers to produce the products to my exacting standards while I concentrated on the product development, marketing and distribution aspects of the business. My chocolates eventually became very popular, not only in Australia but also overseas, with clients gifting them to family and friends, and even famous people abroad, who have shared their great reviews.

My commitment to creating memorable chocolate gift experiences led to customers asking for additional luxury gift ideas to complement our chocolate range. As a result, I expanded my range to other unique and memorable gift suggestions, including French flowers and candles.

My Enjoy Dark Chocolate Facebook page had grown to more than 4,500 followers at the time of the trolling attacks.

In 2018, I proudly became a brand partner of Nu Skin, an exceptional global company dedicated to the development and distribution of cutting-edge, science-based beauty and wellbeing technologies. It brings me great joy to provide guidance to my clients and offer mentorship to my international team, helping them make the most of Nu Skin's innovative beauty devices, skincare solutions, anti-aging products, and nutritional supplements. All of these valuable services are delivered through my AgelessYou consultation service[1].

---

[1] https://khuramanarmstrong.com/pages/beauty and https://khuramanarmstrong.com/pages/wellbeing

To promote my Nu Skin business, I have an active social media presence, where I engage with people via Facebook to build my network of customers. I am known within the company and amongst my customers for my excellent customer service, and as a leader who helps others to achieve their goals. I am also proud to actively participate in Nu Skin's Nourish the Children initiative, which helps to feed underprivileged children all around the world.

In the midst of the pandemic in 2020, I launched the Global Storytellers Facebook and Meetup groups as a part of my continuing online marketing studies and business development. The aim of this initiative had been to support people from diverse cultural backgrounds through online networking and business promotion. The first online meeting, titled The Art of Storytelling, took place on 24 September 2020, and the second online meeting was held in October 2020. The initiative was warmly received by people who were in lockdown for an extended period; it provided a fantastic way for them to connect with others during a challenging time.

Prior to the trolling attack, I was successful and very happy in my businesses. I had gained a reputation for my exceptional and uncompromising customer service, which had led to me being invited to give a presentation on my approach to customer service within my Nu Skin business community. My Azerbaijani heritage had played a significant role in the success of my businesses, namely by extending my national culture of generosity and hospitality to my customers. This involved spending countless additional hours hosting people in my home, and going above and beyond what would typically be expected from a beauty consultation.

The success of my business and service was reflected in the outstanding reviews I received. I had earned 5-star ratings on both my Khuraman Armstrong business Facebook page, and my Enjoy Dark Chocolate business Facebook page. In fact, my Enjoy Dark Chocolate Facebook page boasted a greatly appreciated 215 five-star reviews.

Assel Snazell recommends **KhuramanArmstrong.com.**
October 6, 2020 ·

I know Khuraman since she has run her "Enjoy the Dark Chocolate" business. She has always been very prompt on delivering delicious health treats and responding to my email orders. Later on she has helped me with establishing my regular skin routine with Nu Skin products. I am delighted that we have found that works well for my sensitive and problem skin. She has very personal, warm and approachable care to all of her customers. Highly recommend Khuraman if you are after professional advice and support in choosing skin care options.

Khuraman Armstrong and 3 others   1 comment

To sum up, I am a devoted businesswoman who holds deep affection for both her home country and her adopted one, as well as for her businesses and clients. It is beyond my comprehension why someone would spread false information about my personal integrity, the quality of my chocolate products, or the level of customer service provided across all of my businesses. When the online trolling attack first began, I was completely baffled as to what I had done wrong, and why people would target me in this manner. The impact was significant, both on my personal life and my business.

Let it be known that although I am proud to be an Azerbaijani and an Australian, I am by no means a political operative or an 'agent provocateur', as some of my attackers have maliciously suggested to justify their actions.

2. SO WHAT DID I DO TO DESERVE ALL THIS?

Even though the following chapter focuses on a handful of online activities I participated in over a three-month period in 2020, it is important to emphasise that ever since starting my businesses in 2015, as well as during the period discussed, I published dozens of posts and comments every month across multiple social media platforms, and participated in many online forums, all positively championing my community contributions, and promoting many different products and services across my skin and beauty, wellbeing, chocolate, and luxury-gifting businesses, but I have never posted about politics. This fact highlights how, regardless of the frequency and positivity of your online presence, it only takes one misinterpreted post to bring the trolls crashing down upon you.

SOME BACKGROUND

My home country of Azerbaijan, along with Armenia and Georgia, sits in the South Caucasus region on the crossroads between Europe and Asia. It is a region with rich culture, delicious cuisine, and amazing nature, yet a rather difficult history. Since the beginning of the 1990s, Azerbaijan found itself in increasing conflict with its neighbour Armenia due to the territorial claims of Armenia over several territories of Azerbaijan.

This culminated when, at the time the Soviet Union was falling apart, the armed forces of Armenia invaded Azerbaijan and occupied almost 20% of its lands, including the city of Shusha. This illegal occupation, which claimed many innocent lives, forced more than 1 million people out of their homes and left many cities and villages destroyed, lasted for almost 30 years. (I cover this conflict in more detail in Appendix II)

Countless meetings and mediation efforts by international organizations regrettably yielded no results. Meanwhile, military provocations were getting more frequent and severe, along with toughened rhetoric by the Armenian leadership. Thus, in response to yet another armed attack by the military forces of Armenia in late September 2020, Azerbaijan had to undertake a counter-offensive operation to protect its civilian population. The combat actions that followed went down in history as the 44 Days War and resulted in the liberation of the territories of Azerbaijan that had been held under military occupation for decades.

As an Azerbaijani, I am obviously pleased to have our lands liberated, including my grandfather's hometown of Kalbajar, but my overwhelming emotion is one of sadness for the families of the thousands of casualties on both sides.

I hope the communities of both countries can now find solace and healing, and forge a path to a future filled with harmony and mutual respect, no matter where we live in the world.

But what does this have to do with my trolling and defamation, you may ask?

ECHOES OF SHUSHA

In September 2018, two years before the attacks on me began, I created a new chocolate, which combined vibrant notes of red, wild strawberry pâte de fruits with the earthy notes of green pistachio marzipan. It was a confectionery delight that tantalised the tastebuds and stirred the soul, but initially I could not grant it a name as I had done with my other chocolate creations, each of which bears a unique identity, like the Siberian Burst or the French Affair. The name would come in due course, but in the beginning the chocolate had to speak for itself.

In October 2018, as I contemplated what to name my latest chocolate creation, a childhood memory suddenly flashed in my mind like a burst of lightning. It was of a road trip I took with my father through the breathtaking region of Shusha, with its rolling green hills and terracotta rooftops. As we drove, a melodious voice singing mugham filled the air. We pulled over and saw a young boy strolling carefree along the road, his voice echoing through the region.

Before its occupation by Armenia on 8 May 1992, Shusha was a cultural centre of Azerbaijan, renowned for its talented singers, composers and artists. The people of this region are believed to have a natural gift for music. It is said of this region that 'every child can sing before they learn to speak'. Shusha is particularly renowned for its mastery of mugham, and is often referred to as 'the music conservatory of the Caucasus'.

This memory inspired me to name my latest chocolate creation Echoes of Shusha, as I wanted to evoke both the stunning scenery and the beautiful music that still echoes in my mind. At the time, I shared the story behind the naming of my creation in a Facebook post, intentionally leaving out any reference to Shusha's occupation.

Like most of my posts, this story received warm support and, until the trolling attack started in July 2020, I had been promoting and selling Echoes of Shusha as part of my wider range of branded chocolates, without any complaints or criticism of its name from any customers. It was a top seller, not only because it was vegan, but also due to its delectable taste, which isn't always the case with vegan products.

RUSSIAN INFLUENCE COOKING SHOW

In May 2020 I was contacted by the executive producer of the *Russian Influence* TV show (now known as *Foreign Influence*), who asked if she could interview me for an episode of her show. She said she had been following me online for a while and liked how I was always positively presenting the culture, traditions and cooking of Azerbaijan.

The filming took place on 21 June 2020 in my house, where I discussed several aspects of Azerbaijani cooking and culture, as well as the background of my chocolate business. Again, at no time did I discuss the Armenian-occupied territories. Talk about walking on eggshells.

On 23 July 2020, the program posted an advertisement on the Russian Women's Network Melbourne Facebook group, promoting the upcoming episode with a short one-minute teaser video, and the show aired on the following dates:

- The Russian Influence's YouTube channel on 27 July 2020[2]
- Channel 31 Melbourne and Geelong, also on 27 July 2020
- Foxtel Aurora channel on 26 August 2020

Even before the show aired, hate comments from Armenian group members started to appear on the Russian Women's Network Melbourne Facebook group under the promotional post and trailer.

This is the true flavour of your chocolate. Shameless people! Sell them to your brothers from ISIS! If you are spreading such lies your hands are as much covered in blood as the hands of those terrorists who support your army!	This is redoculius!!! Karabakh is NOT Azerbaijian and neither is Kata (Gata) !!!! Do you homework before promoting incorrect information!!

---

[2] https://ich.unesco.org/en/RL/dolma-making-and-sharing-tradition-a-marker-of-cultural-identity-01188

stop mediating and inciting international terrorism. The author of this ugly post should be in prison for inciting international discord and nationalistic cases! You will be held accountable for ugly programs and interviews. We live in Australia! Australian transmissions, interviews and posts are strictly punished by law! You support a candid criminal! We have sent numerous complaints to your editorial office personally, because it is a crime! You will answer the strictness of the law with your close friend Hunamat! Shameful!

Dear group members, this episode is only about food. It expresses no political opinions other than what tastes great. I understand people have broader emotions but in the interest of tolerance we need to remember that this is just about food. We hope that all countries can enjoy food from anywhere in the world in the hope that food brings us together instead of driving us apart.

Love   2y   ⭕🔵😆 10

Despite the reassuring response from the show's producer, negative comments continued to appear on the Russian Women's Network group page until, at my request, the Facebook group administrator eventually took down the defamatory posts. But not before potentially 7,500 group members saw them, including my customers and other group members who reached out to me with screenshots. It should be noted that despite breaking the group's rules, the haters were allowed to remain in the group. Even two years later, I still receive questions from members of the group regarding the incident.

Unfortunately, the situation only escalated when the full show was released on *Russian Influence*'s YouTube channel in late July 2020. Despite over two hundred positive comments about the show, the Armenian trolls found the video and began their usual negative rants.

Coca Cola is older than Azerbaijan but claims all the traditional food from Armenia what a joke

👍 6 👎   Reply

▼ 3 replies

Most of the food and traditions in this video are Armenian. Azerbaijan didn't exist 103years ago. The people in that region are a mix of Turks and Persians who are claiming a newly created nation and country by convincing you that these are their traditions.

👍 3   👎   Reply

▼ 15 replies

This video disgusts me... it's a cultural appropriation of traditional Armenian Culture and Food. This woman tell tails of Azeri 'culture' but what she states in particular with the food is Armenian. This is the Azeri dictators objective to build a story through its education and people of a past that never was... they have taken so much from the Armenians and it's culture and land. Now they say it's theirs... what a joke!

👍 8   👎   Reply

▲   ■ • 15 replies

Foreign_Influence_TV 2 years ago

sorry, I only have two degrees from that little country town University called Melbourne. The hardest thing to open is a closed mind

👍 7   👎   Reply

@Foreign_Influence_TV then I recommend you get a refund because it seems like they didn't teach you about Tigranes the Great and Armenian History dating Before Christ... Or at least to have an open mind and research about Armenian History. If you are Russian and a true Orthodox, then you know very well you're playing Devil's advocate.

👍 2   👎   Reply

I don't thinks she is russian. Russians know the history of Armenian people and always stand in arms with Armenians . Now more than ever

Russian_Influence And what is your degree on? In Armenian culture. You really have no clue if you continue to believe that these dishes are national azeri, that country is about 100 years old where Armenians were a state way before Russia did. Read history, learn history, don't be ignorant

👍   👎   Reply

2 years ago

is not attacking, but Defending. There's a difference. You're making false accusations and claims. And so is this video and the reporter. This channel is not verified, nor is the reporter verified as a "Russian". Don't think I don't see what you're doing here with your "friend" reporter. This video is false. Period.

👍 1   👎   Reply

2 years ago

What a rude and aggressive response.

👍   👎   Reply

2 years ago

no, what's rude is cultural appropriation which is exactly what this video is... Azeri's may make these dishes at home, but these are NOT Azeri cultural dishes... this is more propaganda, something we are all too used to unfortunately

It has since been revealed through my legal proceedings that two things were central to the Armenian outrage towards the *Russian Influence* show: my use of a map of Azerbaijan that displayed the occupied areas, which they deemed offensive and provocative; and my preparation of Karabakh kata and Azerbaijani dolma. They claimed that both of these dishes were Armenian national dishes rather than Azerbaijani.

Although I believe that arguing over recipes is absurd, I will address their objections. Firstly, a quick Google search of any independent maps confirms that Karabakh is, in fact, part of Azerbaijan. Furthermore, the Armenian occupation was no secret, so what I presented was neither offensive nor provocative. Moreover, as the Karabakh region belongs to Azerbaijan, a fact that has been recognised by the whole international community, it is not only logical, but factually correct to consider Karabakh kata to be part of Azerbaijani cuisine.

Furthermore, as I mentioned during the show, dolma is a dish that is prepared and enjoyed by various cultures and nations worldwide, each with their unique ingredients and methods. In this particular instance, I was demonstrating the Azerbaijani style of preparing dolma.

Moreover, extensive research on the origins of dolma has revealed that UNESCO has officially recognised it as part of Azerbaijan's intangible heritage.[3] This significant recognition was granted during the 12th session of the Intergovernmental Committee for the Safeguarding of Intangible Cultural Heritage, held from December 4-9, 2017, on Jeju Island. This endorsement by UNESCO further reinforces the cultural importance of Azerbaijani dolma. Therefore, I am resolute in my position and find no grounds to apologise for celebrating and sharing this cherished aspect of my cultural heritage.

Furthermore, Azerbaijan is rich in a diverse array of intangible heritage, encompassing various cultural practices and traditions. This includes the

---

[3]   https://ich.unesco.org/en/RL/dolma-making-and-sharing-tradition-a-marker-of-cultural-identity-01188

traditional dance Yalli; the art of making flatbread 'lavash' which is shared with Iran, Kazakhstan, Turkey, and Kyrgyzstan; the skillful craftsmanship of Kelaghayi silk headscarves; the traditional Karabakh horse riding game known as Chovgan; and the mesmerizing performance of Azerbaijani Mugham. Additionally, Azerbaijan is known for the Art of Azerbaijani Ashiq, the craftsmanship and performance art of the Tar, a long-necked string musical instrument, as well as the copper craftsmanship of Lahij, and many other noteworthy traditions. The list is extensive, and for those interested, more information can be explored and discovered through the provided link to UNESCO's official source.[4] Azerbaijan's intangible heritage is a testament to the country's rich cultural tapestry and serves as a source of pride and appreciation for its people.

Finally, the troll's absurd suggestions that Azerbaijani people and culture didn't exist until the formation of the Democratic Republic of Azerbaijan in 1918, is absolutely laughable – like we appeared from nowhere. In fact, any objective reading of history shows that Azerbaijani people have ancient traditions of statehood, along with a rich historical past and diverse cultural legacy, that go back at least 1000 years.

Moreso, engaging in arguments over food or cultural practices seems unnecessary when the true beauty lies in the diversity and richness of different traditions. Each nation holds its own unique intangible heritage, deserving appreciation and recognition. Instead of engaging in disputes, it is more constructive to foster cultural exchange, understanding, and appreciation among nations, celebrating both the similarities and differences that make our world vibrant and culturally diverse.

Fortunately, the negative comments were limited to *Russian Influence*'s YouTube channel. Despite being shocked and disappointed by the negative comments, I eventually put them behind me and resumed promoting my various businesses, including my Enjoy Dark Chocolate business. This was

---

[4]   https://ich.unesco.org/en/lists?text=&country%5b%5d=00018&multinational=3#tabs

important, as I was preparing to resume chocolate production following Melbourne's extended Covid-19 lockdowns, which were scheduled to lift in late October 2020.

DON'T MENTION THE WAR

On October 10, 2020, I received a Facebook reminder about the creation of my Echoes of Shusha chocolate two years prior. Wanting to promote one of my favourite and most popular chocolates, I posted the following statement on both my personal and business pages. Given that the 44 Days War was raging at the time, causing tensions between the Armenian and Azerbaijani communities around the globe, I went out of my way to be conciliatory, believing then, as I do today, that my words were measured and diplomatic. Unfortunately, as events have since proved, simply mentioning Shusha was enough to send the Armenian trolls into overdrive.

'Today is exactly 2 years since my Australian chocolate company, Enjoy Dark Chocolate, launched 'Echoes of Shusha' chocolate that I dedicated to a beautiful region in my homeland, Azerbaijan. Shusha is the Crown Jewel, an ancient culture centre of Azerbaijan. Also renowned for its spectacular landscapes, Shusha is best known for the mastery of its singers, composers, and artists, talents which seem universally given to the gentle peoples of this region, of whom it is said their children sing before they learn to speak.

At the time I launched my chocolate I avoided any direct reference to the fact that Shusha, along with 20% of Azerbaijan, has been under illegal occupation of Armenia for almost 30 years. Likewise I avoided the subject of occupation during our recent 'Azerbaijani culture and cuisine' program aired on National TV of Australia. However, the dedication of my chocolate reflected the deep connection Azerbaijanis still feel for their lands and the collective hurt that this unresolved occupation causes our country. I share this today, not to comment directly on the current war to liberate Azerbaijani lands, but rather to acknowledge the hurt that all unresolved occupation causes the rightful traditional owners of all occupied lands.

Shusha lives in our hearts and echoes in our souls, and I dream of the day when I can return to Shusha and share my chocolates with our people returning to their homes.'

KhuramanArmstrong.com
October 10, 2020 · ⚙

Today is exactly 2 years since my Australian chocolate company Enjoy Dark Chocolate launched "Echoes of Shusha" (⭐ Şuşanın sədaları⭐) chocolate that I dedicated to a beautiful region in my homeland Azerbaijan 🇦🇿

Shusha is the Crown Jewel, an ancient culture centre of Azerbaijan.

Also renowned for its spectacular landscapes, Shusha is best known for the mastery of its singers, composers, and artists, talents which seem universally given to the gentle peoples of this region, of whom it is said their children sing before they learn to speak.

At the time I launched my chocolate I avoided any direct reference to the fact that Shusha, along with 20% of Azerbaijan, has been under illegal occupation of Armenia for almost 30 years.

Likewise I avoided the subject of occupation during our recent "Azerbaijani culture and cuisine" program aired on National TV of Australia.

However, the dedication of my chocolate reflected the deep connection Azerbaijanis still feel for their lands and the collective hurt that this unresolved occupation causes our country.

I share this today, not to comment directly on the current war to liberate Azerbaijani lands, but rather to acknowledge the hurt that all unresolved occupation causes the rightful traditional owners of all occupied lands.

Shusha lives in our hears and echoes in our souls, and I dream of the day when I can return to Shusha and share my chocolates with our people returning to their homes.

#Shusha #KarabakhisAzerbaijan #enjoydarkchocolate #azerbaijan

3. THE MOB ATTACK

Within hours of publishing, the post was seen by some particularly aggressive Armenian activists who, by their own admission, were angry about the war so they were taking out their frustration on me. Rallying their extended Facebook network, they launched a vicious, racially motivated mob attack against my businesses, particularly my chocolate business, and myself.

This included relentlessly attacking my personal Facebook page, my Khuraman Armstrong Facebook business page, and my Enjoy Dark Chocolate Facebook business page, leaving more than eighty vile comments, fake reviews, and online and phone threats of violence against myself. This was all amplified by a deluge of calls and messages of concern and support from my clients, business colleagues and friends, who saw the attack play out in real time online.

VILE POSTS AND COMMENTS

Hi khuraman. Do you know that you beloved Homeland is being parted right now

5000 of your sheep is dead, we killed them

Congratulations!!!

There is more to come 😃

Khuraman Armstrong you better stop all your lie propaganda! You poison people! You are a criminal and international terrorist! You have been reported to the special offices and investigation started!

███████████ Terrible person! Shame shame shame! Close your chocolate story! It's finished business! We will call police and you will be jailed as an international terrorist! Delete your chocolate story right now! We demand! 😱

██████████████ terrible! The worst on the world! Full of poison and blood! 🤮

It is a lie! This uneducated woman uses her chocolate for political reasons! The quality of her products is awful! Terrible quality, expired products. The full dirt! Horror, nightmare and poison! Never, under no circumstances buy it or give it to your kids! She poisons people!

███████████ Враньё! Это безграмотная женщина использует свой шоколад для политических нападок вместо того, чтоб заняться качеством своего товара- безобразное качество, просроченные продукты. Сплошная грязь! Ужас и кошмар, отрава! Никогда ни при каких обстоятельствах не покупайте и не давайте своим детям! Она готовит отраву!

████████
You are just as ignorant as the rest of the world
#StopAzerbaijaniAggression
#IStandWithARTSAKH
#ArtsakhStrong
Long live Armenia 🇦🇲
Long live Artsakh
We will win ❤️💙🧡

████████
Now everybody watch! Isn't it the best proof of her real intentions? Nationalism and international terrorise! Chocolate has nothing to do with her source of living!

...., she advertises her awful chocolate when so much is happening around. She is only thinking about her own interests. Why should we buy chocolate from Azerbaijanis? What, Melbourne doesn't have other chocolates? Buy from Azerbaijani? Only in terrible dream! She is awful provocateur. What the hell? How many Azeris in Melbourne? Burn in hell chocolate, full of poison and crime.

Azeri dictators objective to build a story through its education and people of a past that never was... they have taken so much from the Armenians and it's culture and land. Now they say it's theirs... what a joke!

██████████████ и рекламировать свой поганый шоколад, когда там такое творится! Как можно для своих меркантильных интересов- толкануть конфетульки(как будто в Мельбурне больше нет конфет, только у азеров должны мы покупать! Кошмарный сон)- нажимать на такие больные точки! Я же говорю- страшный провокатор! Какого черта? Сколько в этом Мельбурне азеров? К черту этот шоколад, полный яда и преступлений!

█████████████████ it's not century ago. It's going right now! Watch the news! And this provocative woman didn't call her product Echos of Azerbaijan or Echos of Baku! She deliberately calls it that name to provoke people as this is her job. She covers her real intentions by sweets. Her job is international provocations. A real businesswoman will call it somehow Melbourne fantasy or something else if that would be her source for living. So correspondingly she did it all on purpose as the provocation is her job. You can't imagine how many posts and reviews she has deleted! She doesn't care about her product, she cares about such kind of international tension . A smart business woman will care about her product to be sold and will avoid all the political confrontation. But she does it on purpose. A presentation of the product speaks for itself!

the whore

troll azeri, children murderer, isis contributor, we are lodging formal complaint at the lawsuit, you are promoting ISIS and terrorism as your president doing,

erdoghan kidnapped 3 teenagers from Afrin and conveyed to azerbaijan to kill innocent Armenians, we have their names.

You are so ignorant it's not funny. Read and understand the history of Artsakh not your absolute crap. This is Armenia and has been for over 6000 years. Not your murderous liars. You are not even from this area. Go back to your trees. Go back to where you came from you murderous bunch of animals. Shame on you animals. You want to fight, fight your own battles and see where you land up. Cowards. Getting assistance from your murderous pathetic turks and others including the lousy Pakistan an... See More

supports ISIS/terrorism/azerbaijan, by selling her poisoned disgusting chocolates, just be aware, every penny you pay here goes to funding terrorism, to the killer to beheads innocent people in France, Syria, Armenia, such as ramil safarov. who beheaded NATO solider at 3.00 am while the victim was sleeping.
https://www.theguardian.com/world/2020/may/29/clarifying-the-case-of-ramil-safarov

let her chocolate burn in hell!

FAKE NEGATIVE REVIEWS

As hurtful as these posts were, I ultimately knew I could delete most of them once I assessed my legal options. However, it was the fake reviews that really hurt the most. In fact, after I began deleting some of the posts, one of the ringleaders of the attack explicitly directed others to write negative reviews, probably knowing that I couldn't delete those.

> ████████████ She is deleting all the comments! Write the longer reviews!

These reviews had a direct impact on my business rating, which had previously been perfect, with only 5-star ratings for both my Khuraman Armstrong and Enjoy Dark Chocolate business pages.

As someone who takes pride in providing exceptional customer service, the drop to two stars was soul-destroying. It felt like all the hard work and dedication I had put into my business was being undone by the fake reviews. The negative impact on my business, and to my reputation, was very emotionally draining.

> ████████████ doesn't recommend Khuraman Armstrong.
> 19h
>
> Disgusting people to deal with. Hiding behind chocolate supporting terrorism.

> ████████████ doesn't recommend Khuraman Armstrong.
> 1d
>
> Disgusting! How can you post such rubbish while trying to promote your chocolates. Hurtful and shameful.

doesn't recommend Enjoy Dark Chocolate.

5d

Not sure if they know what the real chocolate tastes like- for a beginner they're doing an ok job but for a business - SOS

doesn't recommend Khuraman Armstrong.

2d

Disgusting person spreading hate and supporting a country that kills innocent lives and supports terrorism.

doesn't recommend Khuraman Armstrong.

19h

false information, she supports terrorism through her fake "chocolates ", watch out Melbourne!

doesn't recommend Khuraman Armstrong.

1h

Worst chocolate, worst customer service 😡😡😡

doesn't recommend Khuraman Armstrong

5h

all the positive posts are just pro Azerbaijani ones. doubt they've tried anything

doesn't recommend Enjoy Dark Chocolate.

5d

Chocolate was not dark enough. Did not enjoy

doesn't recommend Khuraman Armstrong.

1d

The azeri ability to lie is injected in this chocolate. Gross!

doesn't recommend Khuraman Armstrong.
18h

Horrible and absolutely shameful

doesn't recommend **Khuraman Armstrong**.
Just now

Beautiful lyrical liar, who uses some sweets to make terrorist statements and support azerbaijani aggression during war times.

doesn't recommend Khuraman Armstrong.
3m

Do not support this person. spreading hate against people. Disgusting! 🤮

doesn't recommend Khuraman Armstrong.
7h

Racist, homophobic, xenophobic, very abusive woman who supports violence, do not purchase her chocolates as her profits support terrorism.

doesn't recommend Khuraman Armstrong.
3d

Biased politics instead of chocolates.

doesn't recommend Enjoy Dark Chocolate.
5d

If by 'Enjoy' you mean 'worse than laxatives' and 'projectile sharting' then sure.... very enjoyable 🤢. Avoid at all costs.

doesn't recommend Khuraman Armstrong.
2d

Disgusting

doesn't recommend Khuraman Armstrong.
23h

Stilling recipes, telling lies, promoting aggressor country.

EVEN MORE LIES

After enduring several days of this ordeal, I finally gathered the courage to confront some of the offenders. However, despite my efforts, they continued to persist with their harassment. I was taken aback by their audacity and willingness to flat-out lie, even when challenged.

doesn't recommend Khuraman Armstrong.

The chocolate I ordered never came and got lost in transit. I kindly asked Khuraman for a refund however no one ever got back to me. After numerous attempts I gave up. I would give 0 stars for customer service. Wouldn't recommend.

Khuraman Armstrong You are a liar! You have never bought my product. This is nothing but racial vilification which is illegal in Australia.

Like · Reply · Message · 3h · Edited

Khuraman Armstrong How can you accuse me of being a liar???? Rude. Just proves my point on bad customer service.

Like · Reply · Message · 2h

Khuraman Armstrong Then send me proof that you purchased my product!

Like · Reply · 2h

doesn't recommend Khuraman Armstrong.

26m ·

Deletes all the constructive criticism from her product comments. I highly doubt after this how her chocolates or anything she does qualify, if she is not evolving and working for her customers! Poor very ignorant behavior for an entrepreneur!

Wouldn't recommend at all

> **Khuraman Armstrong** You never bought my chocolate. Get off my page you whining Armenian. Had enough of you
>
> Like · Reply · Message · 23m   1
>
>> Khuraman Armstrong yeah and i never will. By your product i meant the terrorism that you support! And of course Azeri "lady" this is your customer service. The world had more than enough of YOU!! Terrorists
>>
>> Like · Reply · Message · 9m

---

doesn't recommend Khuraman Armstrong.

1d ·

Buyer beware, terrible customer service. No intention of resolving issues, a little rude and aggressive. Don't waste your time.

👍😆😠 4

> **Khuraman Armstrong** You are liar ▇ You have never purchased our products.
>
> Like Reply 2d

> Actually I have Khuraman, under our business. It's a shame you're calling your customers liars. 👍
>
> Like Reply Message 1d

>> **Khuraman Armstrong** Whats is your business name? You still didnt show me the proof, as you are liar. You will be responsible for your lies.
>>
>> Like Reply 25m

>> Khuraman Armstrong yeah I think not😄
>>
>> Like Reply Message 23m

PHONE THREATS

As if the hurtful posts and reviews weren't enough, I was also subjected to six threatening calls, which were frankly terrifying, and had a deep and long-lasting impact on me. The offenders had crossed a dangerous line with their actions, and I was genuinely afraid for my safety and that of my family. The whole experience was extremely distressing.

To give you a sense of how extreme the threats were, this is a transcript from one of the calls that I recorded:

Me: Hello, who are you?
Caller: I am anti-terrorist group manager …
Me: From where?
Caller: … and we are going to sue people like you, fucking Azerbaijani, the terrorist, the ISIS, the ISIS founder and supplier.
Me: Who are you?
Caller: Just be sure that every [blood] is being checked in Syria by your terrorists. You and your [inaudible] and we are working on it. You will be accountable for every [blood]. You are a terrorist …
Me: What is your name?
Caller: … of Azerbaijan, beheading people. Beheading people, you conniving cunt, beheading people and you are supporting them. Your product is now being published in every newspaper in Australia, just so people know who you are. You're a motherfucker. You are a murderer.

The other calls also included threats to behead me, so clearly I took these very seriously and immediately called the police, which, as you will read shortly, resulted in an incomprehensible response.

In the following two weeks, I had to block more than fifty different Facebook profiles. All were people I had never met, and they certainly weren't customers of my businesses. Eventually the mob moved on, but by the time the dust settled, around the end of October 2020, I was totally shattered and scared.

This feeling of utter vulnerability was compounded by the realisation that none of the authorities to whom I had reported the attack—including the local and federal police, two online protection agencies, and Facebook themselves—was willing or able to assist, which to this day still disgusts me, as I explain in detail in the following chapters.

And, just like the *Russian Influence* show outcry, I still struggle to reconcile such rage against my innocuous post. However, based on some of the defences put forward over the course of my legal action, it would appear that their objections centred on the following:

- The post was made by an Azerbaijani woman.
- I dared to name a chocolate in honour of the Azerbaijan city of Shusha, which Armenians claim as their own 'Shushi'.
- I dared to speak about the hurt experienced by the rightful owners of occupied lands.
- I dared hope that our occupied lands would be returned to Azerbaijan soon.

How utterly petty and unjust.

THE OFFENDERS

So, who were these trolls? It was obvious that the attacks were coordinated by a few Armenian extremists firing up their minions, who happily followed along, mostly without any originality or thought of the consequences.

The main ringleader, who shall remain nameless, seemed to be everywhere; she was virtually an online stalker who appeared to sit on my pages 24/7. She made several of her own horrible and threatening posts, as well as commenting on and liking many of the other negative posts and reviews.

Despite her denials, I believed her to be one of the main protagonists, because at the same time that she was writing her own messages across my Facebook pages, I started to get all the other negative posts and reviews, as well as life-threatening phone calls. The callers all used similar rhetoric: they called me names, and accused me of lying about my chocolate and being a terrorist.

Eventually I began checking the Facebook pages of those who were attacking me and discovered that long before my attack they all had one thing in common: an apparent hatred of Turks and Azerbaijanis.

I was horrified to come across multiple threads on their profile pages where they discussed punishing Azerbaijanis in different countries based solely on their nationality. Even more concerning was the fact that they had published the phone numbers and addresses of some of their targets. Given that they already had my phone number and address, and had already begun making life-threatening phone calls against me, this discovery filled me with an overwhelming sense of fear for my safety. The situation felt incredibly dangerous, and left me feeling vulnerable and uncertain about what might happen next.

It's truly frightening to realise that there are people, including many living among us here in Australia, harbouring such extreme levels of hatred. The fact that these individuals are willing to target and threaten others based solely on their nationality is deeply troubling, and goes against the principles of acceptance and inclusivity that I strive to uphold in my daily activities.

And, for the record, apart from the individuals who attacked me, and their endless propaganda and falsehoods regarding the conflict, I have no grievances against Armenians. In Azerbaijan my family and I lived happily with many Armenians as our neighbours, at least until many of them mysteriously sold up their homes and businesses and returned to Armenia just prior to the 1992 occupation by Armenia of the Azerbaijani territories. Clearly, they had got the memo.

SADLY, I AM NOT ALONE

As I've just shared, the majority of the attacks on me were of a defamatory nature, where the perpetrators were trying to harm my personal and professional reputation by telling outright lies. However, trolling takes many different forms which is why so many people report being targeted. For example, trolling:

- can target race, culture, religion, gender, sexual orientation, disability, fame, politics, sporting prowess, and even age
- manifests as abuse, ridicule, harassment, threats, bribery, or defamation
- often aims to silence debate or discussion as much as it aims to provokes arguments, emotional reactions, or hatred
- can come just as easily from people you know as from those you don't
- often incites a mob mentality and subsequent group 'pile on'
- is just as prevalent within smaller interest or community groups as it is within geopolitical commentary and debates.

So nobody is immune. In fact, research from the Australian eSafety Commissioner confirms that approximately 5% of all online users report experiencing direct personal cyberbullying each year – see **Appendix III** at the end of this book for a detailed breakdown of this statistic.

When you extrapolate this ratio, even to Facebook's user base alone, this equates to more than **200 million** people globally experiencing cyberbullying annually. That is a staggering number and clearly a social scourge that needs to be addressed. Worse still, I have seen reports citing cyberbullying as the root cause of an average of 10 suicides each week in Australia. This is a horrible waste of life, comparable to our national road toll: look at how much authorities spend on curbing the road toll, so why not cyberbullying?

To make matters worse, research suggests that trolls often try to downplay the impact of their behaviour, often claiming that they were "only joking", or that anyone who's upset by their posts or comments is "overreacting" or needs to "toughen up", none of which could be further from the truth.

This is why I have made it my mission to actively promote online safety for everyone by advocating for an urgent change in online behaviour, and for greater regulatory protection, the reasons for which you are about to read.

4. THE HELP THAT NEVER CAME

Immediately after the posts began in October 2020, I started looking for ways to stop the attack, to have the negative posts and reviews removed, and to send a message to the offenders that this was against the law and not acceptable. Initially, I would have been happy for Facebook to simply remove the posts, and for the police or regulators to send a stern warning notice to the offenders. What a forlorn hope that turned out to be.

THE POLICE

I contacted Victoria Police on Sunday, 18 October to report the online abuse. Following the call, my husband Graeme also sent an email to the assigned officer with the same screenshots that I have included in this book, but unredacted so the police could see the actual profiles of the offenders. To our utter surprise and disbelief, they promptly concluded that 'no offenses have been identified', as can be seen below. I was stunned. Despite sending a follow-up email seeking clarification, I have not received a response from Victoria Police to this day.

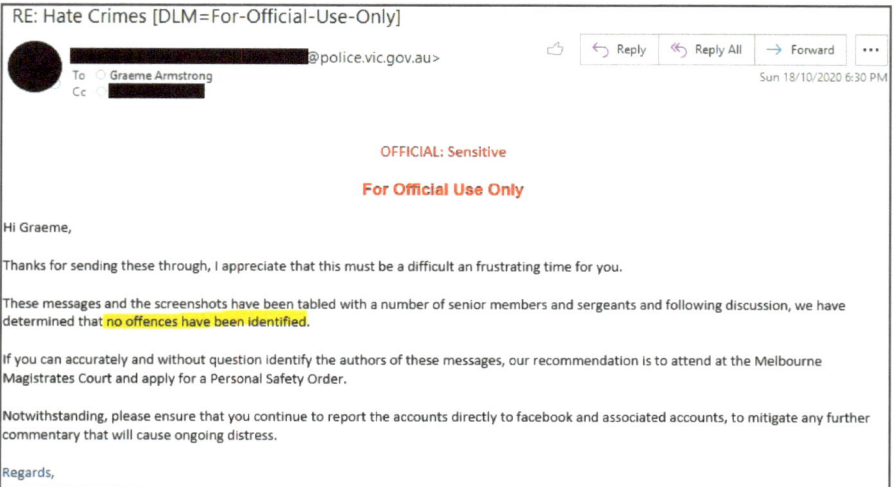

RE: Hate Crimes [DLM=For-Official-Use-Only]

@police.vic.gov.au>

To ○ Graeme Armstrong
Cc ○

👍 ↩ Reply ↩ Reply All → Forward ⋯
Sun 18/10/2020 6:30 PM

OFFICIAL: Sensitive

For Official Use Only

Hi Graeme,

Thanks for sending these through, I appreciate that this must be a difficult an frustrating time for you.

These messages and the screenshots have been tabled with a number of senior members and sergeants and following discussion, we have determined that no offences have been identified.

If you can accurately and without question identify the authors of these messages, our recommendation is to attend at the Melbourne Magistrates Court and apply for a Personal Safety Order.

Notwithstanding, please ensure that you continue to report the accounts directly to facebook and associated accounts, to mitigate any further commentary that will cause ongoing distress.

Regards,

Then the phone threats began. After receiving the first threatening phone call at 10.45 pm on Sunday, 18 October, we called 000. A first constable and three uniformed colleagues came to our home at 11.15 pm. While they were present, the last of the six threatening phone calls was received. After hearing the phone threat firsthand, and reviewing the online trolling, the first constable and his colleagues confirmed that they believed an offence had occurred. They assured us that they would coordinate with the constable and sergeant who sent the above email, and that someone would contact us with regard to coming to the police station and making a statement.

After not hearing from anyone over the following five days, at 10.30 am on Friday, 23 October I attended Melbourne West Police Station to make a statement and secure a case number. The senior constable on the desk asked me to explain my situation. He quickly dismissed my evidence as a civil matter and said the police 'aren't trained to deal with cybercrime'. He also referred us to the Cyber Abuse website, on which we had already lodged a complaint.

To persist, I provided the senior constable with the Facebook profile pages of Armenians residing in Melbourne who had not only left negative comments on my social media pages, but also posted calls to action against other Azerbaijanis around the world. These posts included sharing the phone numbers and addresses of Azerbaijani individuals in various countries, urging other Armenians to locate and physically harm them. Naturally I was concerned about the danger these fellow Melbournians posed but, regrettably, the senior constable did not take my concerns seriously.

And sadly, that's where Victoria Police's assistance started and finished. I have never heard back from them about my direct reports, and nor have I had any response to my subsequent report to the Australian Cyber Security Centre (more on this below).

Frankly, I find this dismissive attitude completely unacceptable. If someone vandalised physical premises by painting profane graffiti all over the shopfront, or tried to burn the business down, the police would be all over it. But because the very same things happen in a digital context, they don't want to know about it, even though both scenarios cause the exact same harm to the proprietor's livelihood.

My case was also raised with the Australian Federal Police via the Azerbaijan embassy in Canberra, but just like with Victoria Police, we never heard back from them either. I felt alone, vulnerable, and unprotected.

ONLINE-SAFETY REGULATORS

On Sunday, 18 October I also reported my attack to the Australian Cyber Security Centre via their website. Sadly, their only response was to refer the matter straight back to Victoria Police.

From: ReportCyber NoReply <noreply@report.cyber.gov.au>
Sent: Sunday, 18 October 2020 4:43 PM
To: Enjoy Dark Chocolate ▓▓▓▓▓▓▓▓▓▓▓▓▓▓▓▓
Subject: We have received your completed ReportCyber submission CIRS-20201018▓▓

Australian Government
Australian Signals Directorate

ACSC Australian Cyber Security Centre

Your ReportCyber Receipt

Thank you for reporting. The reference number for this report is: **CIRS-20201018▓▓**. You can provide this number to financial institutions or other organisations as proof that a report has been submitted to police via ReportCyber at cyber.gov.au/report.

For matters requiring urgent Police attention, contact (000).

For Crisis Support, contact Lifeline (13 11 14); Beyond Blue (1300 224 636); or Kids Helpline (1800 551 800).

Your report has been referred to Victoria Police for assessment. The information in the report is usually sufficient for Victoria Police to complete their assessment. Should further information be required to assist in completing the assessment, Victoria Police will contact you directly.

You will be notified by Victoria Police when the assessment is complete and advised of the outcome. Please note Victoria Police does not reply to further enquiries regarding a report that is under assessment. To do so would delay the assessment process, as staff would need to use valuable time to provide updates rather than complete their assessments.

Due to the complex nature of enquiries undertaken as part of the assessment process, it is not uncommon not to hear from Victoria Police for at least 12 weeks. If there is an immediate threat to life or risk of harm, please call 000.

Based on the information you have provided; someone is bullying you online. This could be a criminal offence.

Ever the optimist, I hoped this report might land with a different, better-trained Victoria Police team but as I mentioned, we never heard from Victoria Police or ACSC again.

We also reported our case to the eSafety Commissioner, but got a similarly unhelpful response, effectively asking us to wait more than a year before legislation changes meant they might be able to help.

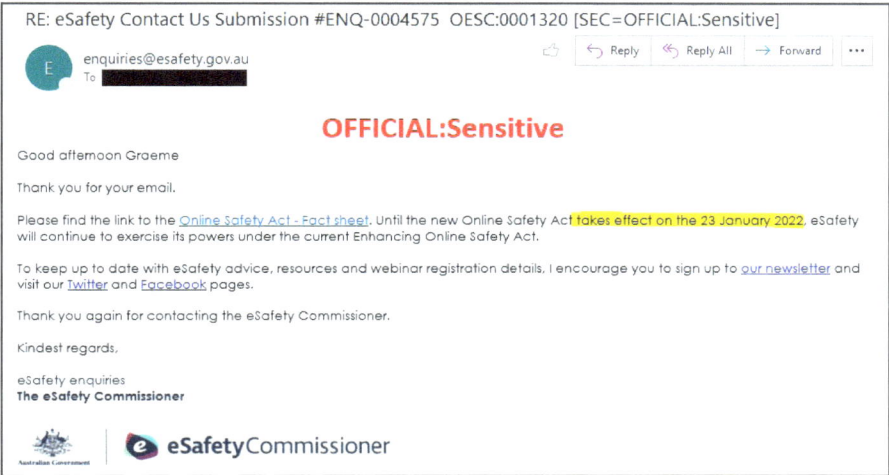

I'm not an e-safety-legislation expert, but my quick read of their current website still doesn't suggest they have the blanket powers I believe necessary to properly protect everyone online, but more on that later.

FACEBOOK

Over the week of 17 October 2020, I reported more than thirty of the most abusive comments and fake reviews to Facebook via their in-built abuse-reporting feature (explained in more detail in Appendix I, **The First Twenty-Four Hours**). However, inexplicably, Facebook did not remove anything, at all, claiming that none of the posts violated their 'community standards'.

What sort of community standards does Facebook have?

You anonymously reported ▮▮▮▮▮▮▮▮▮▮▮▮ **'s post for displaying hate speech.**

UPDATED

Thanks for your feedback
Sunday, October 18, 2020 at 2:01 AM

Thanks for your report - you did the right thing by letting us know about this. The post was reviewed, and though it doesn't go against one of our specific **Community Standards**, we understand that it may still be offensive to you and others. No one should have to see posts they consider hateful on Facebook, so we want to help you avoid things like this in the future.

From the list above, you can block ▮▮▮▮▮▮▮▮▮▮ directly, or you may be able to unfriend or unfollow them. If you unfollow them, you'll stay friends on Facebook but you won't see their posts in your News Feed.

We know these options may not apply to every situation, so please let us know if you see something else you think we should review. You may also consider using Facebook to speak out and educate the community around you. Counter-speech in the form of accurate information and alternative viewpoints can help create a safer and more respectful environment.

Not satisfied with their response, and believing it was likely determined by some AI tool, I appealed Facebook's decision.

Today at 3:54 PM
Our reply

You requested a review of the comment. We'll send an update once our review team has taken another look.

But even the humans took no action. Unbelievable!

Today at 5:05 PM

We didn't take down ▆▆▆▆▆▆▆▆ **comment**

Khuraman, we reviewed the comment that you reported and found ==that it doesn't go against any of our Community Standards==. For this reason we didn't take the comment down.

We keep our review process as fair as possible by using the same **Community Standards** to review reports.

While we've decided not to take this comment down, we understand that you don't like it. We recommend that you hide the comment or unfollow, unfriend or block the person who posted it.

However, there is more to the story. Feeling frustrated by the lack of action taken by the authorities, and concerned about what my friends and customers might think of the negative comments and reviews, I decided to post an explanation on social media. I included examples of some of the negative posts to provide context for anyone who had not seen them before.

Khuraman Armstrong
2d

Hello friends and colleagues.

You may well have noticed recent attacks on my Facebook pages by pro-Armenian trolls. Sadly these cowards, most of which don't know me personally nor have ever bought from me, think that attacking my peaceful and non-political personal and business Facebook pages somehow legitimises Armenia's illegal 30 year occupation of Azerbaijan territory, as denounced by countless UN resolutions, and which is currently being liberated by Azerbaijani forces.

No one hates war more than I do, but the lies and hate being spread about me personally, about my businesses including bogus negative reviews, and about the conflict, leaves me no alternative than to speak out in support of the international rights and protections of my Azerbaijan homeland, and to condemn the attempts by these trolls to directly harm my reputation and businesses.

While we work around the clock to block and delete their poisonous posts, some of which are screenshotted below, I trust that that my friends and loyal customers can see through their utter lies and continue to support by businesses and other positive initiatives.

What happened next was unbelievable. After I posted the explanation, one of the trolls reported my post to Facebook, and as a result my account was suspended for three days. Facebook didn't seem to find anything wrong with the original vile posts and reviews, but they had a problem with me re-sharing them as part of my explanation. It was beyond frustrating.

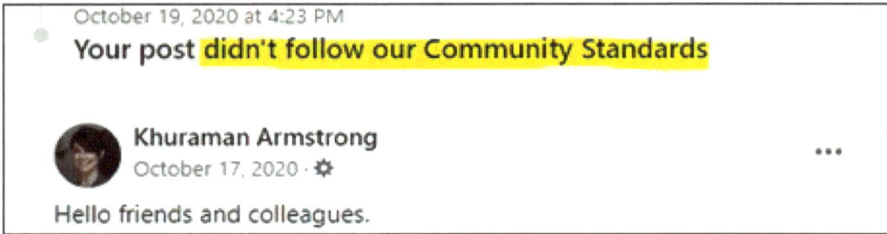

October 19, 2020 at 4:23 PM
Your post didn't follow our Community Standards

Khuraman Armstrong
October 17, 2020 · ⚙

···

Hello friends and colleagues.

Again, I appealed to Facebook, following which they promptly reinstated my account.

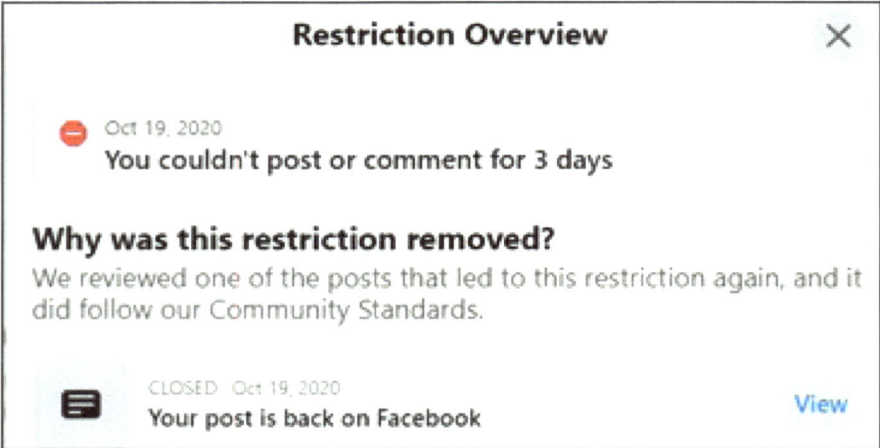

Restriction Overview ✕

● Oct 19, 2020
You couldn't post or comment for 3 days

Why was this restriction removed?
We reviewed one of the posts that led to this restriction again, and it did follow our Community Standards.

CLOSED Oct 19, 2020
Your post is back on Facebook View

Whilst I was happy to have my account back online, and believed that I had got one back on the troll who had reported me, the end result was that Facebook found neither version of the negative posts a problem. This only proves to me that, as an organisation, Facebook has no moral standards, let alone 'community standards'.

Furthermore, without wanting to sound too conspiratorial, at the same time as my attack I was shared some posts, made by Armenians, who claimed to be working at Facebook and 'taking down' all pro-Azerbaijani posts. It is also well known today that if an Azerbaijani even mentions 'Armenia' in a Facebook post, it will lead to that post being automatically removed. So, Facebook would appear to have built-in biases, to say the least.

As annoyed as I was with the lack of action from the police and regulators, for me Facebook's abdication of any responsibility is the greatest travesty of this entire saga.

If Facebook had taken appropriate action by removing blatantly false and defamatory posts and reviews when they were reported, I would have been spared the cost and anguish of the last two and a half years. Therefore, I fully endorse any government or regulatory initiatives aimed at holding platforms such as Facebook accountable. Arguments about free speech, cancel culture, or platform versus publisher are irrelevant in the face of the harm caused to real people by Facebook's lax standards and inaction. The organisation must be held accountable for their role in causing this harm.

THE MEDIA

As word of the attack began to spread among the Azerbaijani community, both here and abroad, I was contacted by a journalist from the Report.az news portal. Unbeknown to me, what I thought was a casual chat between two fellow countrymen was in fact an interview for an online news article.[5] Naturally, had I known our discussion would be published I would have been much more guarded with my answers. Without any editorial control, the end publication didn't accurately reflect our conversation, leaving me to believe that either my Australian accent is stronger than I thought, or, aiming for maximum clicks, the journalist chose to sensationalise the article. Worse still, this article was subsequently used against me by one of the defendants in my legal battle.

---

[5]   https://report.az/bisnes-xeberleri/ermenileri-qorxudan-susanin-sedalari/

I would encourage anyone in my situation to be particularly careful when engaging with the media, no matter how reassuring the attention may seem at the time.

The sad reality is that all my attempts to seek help took weeks of time and effort, produced no assistance at all, led to even more frustration and hurt, and ultimately left me no option but to engage the legal system. It was a disappointing experience, to say the least.

5. MY LEGAL JOURNEY

Given the lack of assistance elsewhere, by November 2020, two months after the attack started and with fake reviews still polluting my business pages, I found myself with no alternative but to turn to the Australian legal system for resolution. I knew that doing so would be expensive, however I hoped that by receiving competent professional advice from an appropriately experienced lawyer, this upfront financial commitment would ultimately achieve an expeditious result by applying quick and decisive legal pressure on the offenders. Wrong again.

Let me emphasise that what follows is not professional legal advice. Rather, it reflects my own experience of pursuing justice through the Australian legal system, which included learning a lot about how fraught the legal system is.

THE BASICS OF DEFAMATION LAW

Although it may seem obvious that the posts and reviews I have shared are defamatory, Australian defamation law, and possibly similar defamation laws elsewhere, is not so straightforward. Defamation law is the same throughout Australia, regardless of state jurisdiction, and is highly technical. In order to prove their case, both the plaintiff (me) and the defendants (the trolls) had to satisfy certain requirements.

To simplify things, I have separated the main considerations by party, but I repeat that this is a brief overview of my understanding only, and should not be taken as professional legal advice.

PLAINTIFF

The plaintiff's case rests on the concept of *imputations*, which essentially link the defendant's published statement with how a reasonable and impartial person would interpret it. In my situation, some of the imputations were quite literal, with the trolls accusing me of being a terrorist or criminal. Other accusations were subtle, such as insinuating that I was a liar or an unpleasant person. Regardless, the first step was to determine which imputations to pursue, and then prove that the defendants had no reasonable cause to make those claims.

Another critical element is *publication*, which means that at least one person other than the plaintiff must have seen or heard the defamatory material. Unlike mainstream media, where it's generally accepted that others have seen or heard defamatory material, publication online is not as readily accepted by the courts. This makes it crucial to gather documented proof of who else saw the offending publications online. This can be done by taking screenshots of texts, messenger conversations, comments, and even emojis. It's essential for the plaintiff to catalogue this evidence in detail, as it will be critical to proving their publication claims. (I cover this process in more detail in Appendix I titled **The First Twenty-Four Hours**.)

Proving both the *publication* and the *effort to minimise impact* can put the plaintiff in a tricky situation. On one hand, leaving the offending publication online can potentially increase the number of witnesses and strengthen the publication case. But on the other hand, the plaintiff is required to show that they have taken reasonable steps to reduce the impact of the attack, meaning the post can't be left online just to maximise the potential damage.

This *effort to minimise impact* also extends to the operation of the business. In my case, I lost my core chocolatier staff, meaning I wasn't able to resume my chocolate business even though I wanted to, and that was quite apart from the severe psychological impact the trolling attacks had on my confidence to be online again. Therefore, as part of my case I had to prove that I had made reasonable efforts to hire new chocolatier staff by supplying evidence of advertising and contract negotiations.

Actuated by malice is another proof point for the plaintiff. This infers that one of the defendant's primary objectives is to unjustly harm your reputation and/or business. Therefore, proving malice is a process of elimination, proving or defeating other proof points required by both the plaintiff and the defence. In my case, it was quite obvious that the offenders wanted to hurt me; however, it was challenging to prove that this was their primary motivation at the time of making the publication.

It should come as no surprise that one of the key things a plaintiff needs to justify is the amount of damages they're seeking. This can include direct costs like lost sales and profits, the cost of fixing a trolled website, expenses for psychological assistance, and other costs that can be proven with an invoice or financial report. Of course, the defendant may try to challenge these submissions, but they're generally easier to prove than indirect costs.

When it comes to indirect costs that can be claimed as damages, there are a few key factors that come into play. One is the devaluation of goodwill in a business, which can be difficult to quantify, but can have a significant impact on the overall value of a company. Another is damage to the plaintiff's personal reputation, which can be even more difficult to prove since they can't produce an invoice to show how much it has cost them. In these cases, the seriousness and breadth of the attacks against the plaintiff become crucial factors in determining the damages they can claim.

Another important consideration is the issue of triviality. If the attacks are seen as minor or insignificant, it may be difficult for the plaintiff to convince a court that they have suffered significant damages.

DEFENDANT

The defendant in a defamation case may have several defences available to them based on the concept of *privilege*. These defences include *absolute privilege*, which applies to statements made in places where anything goes, such as in parliament or in a court; *fair report of proceedings of public concern*, which applies to statements that are a fair report of an important public proceeding, like a court case; and *public documents*, which applies to statements taken from public documents, like records of parliamentary bodies or government documents.

Another type of privilege defence is *qualified privilege*, which applies when the statement is made to provide information that the recipient has a legitimate need to know, and the statement is made without malice.

In addition to privilege defences, the defendant may also rely on the defences of *justification*, where they can prove that their statement was substantially true at the time of publication; *honest opinion*, where the statement is an opinion on a matter of public interest and based on material that is substantially true; and *triviality*, where the statement is unlikely to cause harm.

Although these additional defences were not relevant in my case, they are important considerations for anyone facing a defamation claim.

THE LAWYERS

Before embarking on my search for lawyers, I recognised the importance of identifying the offenders I could and should sue. I understood that I needed to ascertain their true identities, confirm that they resided in Australia, and establish that their online posts were unequivocally defamatory in nature.

Applying my considerable investigative skills, I reluctantly narrowed the list to only seven offenders who met the criteria. I say reluctantly because, while I know seven is a lot of people to sue at once, I really wished it could have been more of the many people who attacked me.

As someone who had never required the services of a lawyer before, I turned to online resources to find an Australian legal expert with specific experience in online defamation cases. To my surprise, my search yielded few results. I even resorted to searching for leads on social media platforms like Facebook—an ironic twist indeed.

Finally, I stumbled upon a newspaper article about a law firm that had recently won a highly publicised online defamation case on behalf of a business owner against her ex-husband and a hairdresser. Though the case involved a somewhat peculiar cast of characters, I assumed the firm's successful prosecution demonstrated their legal expertise with online defamation. Based on this, I decided to contact and subsequently engage them. For reasons that will become clear later, I will not name the firm or any of the lawyers involved. Rather, I'll just refer to them as 'the firm'.

THE PARTNER

Now, I know how professional-services firms, like lawyers, accountants, consultants, etc, work. The more senior and experienced partner will take the initial call, wow you with their illustrious experience and expertise, and then promptly flick you off to one of their underlings to do the actual work. And this is exactly what happened in my case.

The partner of the firm—whom I will call Partner— proudly talked my husband and I through his recent well-publicised win, mentioning several times the $150,000 damages awarded to them. Then, having quickly reviewed the screenshots and other supporting material we provided him, he enthusiastically talked up the strength of my case, confidently inferring that the damages could be multiples of that received by his previous client, given the comparative gravity of the attacks involved. I'll call this the 'initial predicted value'.

To be fair, Partner did preface his initial predicted value with the caveat that 'there are no guarantees in court cases', so I don't want to imply any nefarious intentions on his part. However, I couldn't help but see through his pitch from the very beginning. It reminded me of the real estate industry's practice of 'vendor bashing', where agents inflate the value of a property to secure the listing, only to deflate it when it comes time to close the sale and ultimately collect their commission. With this in mind, and after consulting with my husband, I decided to engage the firm; however, I began to regret that decision almost as soon as the proceedings commenced.

THE ASSOCIATES

As expected, I was quickly handed off to an associate lawyer to begin working on my case. I'll refer to him as First Associate. Looking back, I wish I'd had access to the same advice I now give in Appendix I titled **The First Twenty-Four Hours**, as it would have been clear to me from the beginning that First Associate had very limited knowledge or experience with online defamation, and he especially didn't understand Facebook.

At the time, I was unaware of the intricacies of defamation law, and as a result I had captured screenshots of the offensive publications only, without considering the context in which they were posted, including the original posts, and the subsequent comments and emojis that were associated with them. (If this is all a bit confusing, don't worry, as I explain it in more detail in Appendix I.)

Unfortunately, First Associate failed to request the crucial context upfront, even though he should have immediately identified that my evidence contained these shortcomings. It wasn't until several months later that he sought clarification regarding the type of Facebook page the defamatory publications came from, and whether they were posts, comments or reviews. Shockingly, he wasn't even aware that reviews could only be created on a Facebook business page.

His ignorance in this regard forced us to revisit the horrible posts over and over again, as we pieced together the important additional context required to strengthen our case. The direct and compound result of this incompetence was that the case dragged on for at least a year longer than it should have, causing more stress and costing considerably more money as a result.

CONCERNS NOTICES

My first step in suing for defamation was to issue concerns notices to the offenders. This detailed the publications I believed to be defamatory, the extent of harm caused, and the value of damages I sought. In determining the damages, I essentially assessed the severity and number of publications relative to each other, and apportioned Partner's 'initial predicted value' accordingly. It wasn't particularly scientific, but I had to start somewhere.

Despite the values cited in Partner's initial predicted value, Partner and First Associate immediately began to squirm at the values I nominated. They claimed that their initial predictions assumed a full judgement in court, and that at this stage I should be looking to settle early where possible.

Whilst I accepted this as reasonable advice—I was in no hurry to head to an expensive trial—I was also concerned as to why I should be discounting my claim before even sending the concerns notices. In the end, I compromised by trimming the values a little, mainly just to get the process going. To help keep track, I will call this the first discount.

To be legally considered as 'served', concerns notices should be delivered in writing via registered post or a service agent. Naturally this requires a complete street address, which isn't readily available on Facebook profiles. As part of my initial investigations, I had found reasonably current work or home addresses for the offenders, but I fully expected First Associate to do a proper search using what I assumed were more advanced means available to lawyers. But no, First Associate simply used the addresses I provided, which obviously missed critical details such as an apartment number when it was obvious there should be one.

Not surprisingly, it took several weeks for the concerns notices to reach and be acknowledged by all seven defendants. Eventually they started to respond, mostly via their own lawyers. Regardless of their various rambling justifications, one common complaint was clear, and that was that the concerns notices hadn't been drafted properly. More alarm bells. When I asked First Associate about this, he dismissed the criticism, saying that this was just a normal part of the 'game'. What was clear, however, was that none of the defendants felt in anyway compelled to start negotiating, which was contrary to the way Partner had suggested it would play out.

After several weeks and a lot of back and forth with the other lawyers on the technicalities of the concerns notices, I did start to receive some token offers to settle. While encouraging on one hand, they were insulting on the other, representing a pittance compared with the values stipulated in the concerns notices, and were even further from Partner's initial predicted figures. So I rejected them. But then came the insistence from Partner that I make a counteroffer, in each case of less value than in the concerns notices, to show that I was willing to negotiate, and that this would be an important consideration taken into account by the judge should it go to trial.

Now I had discounted twice before I had seen any real indication that the other parties were serious about settling. But again, I trimmed a little, my second discount. This was more for expedience and to appease my own legal team than from any confidence I felt that this would entice the undeserving defendants. Needless to say, this was a futile exercise: the counteroffers were rejected and the negotiations stopped there.

But one interesting development did occur. Two of the defendants came forward and named a new third party as the author of their defamatory posts. Let me get this straight. You handed your phones to a friend and let them post defamatory reviews on your behalf? How brilliant of you. Not only did you incriminate yourselves but you also just threw your friend under the proverbial bus.

Now, instead of seven defendants, there were eight.

STATEMENTS OF CLAIM

With no settlements in sight, the next step was to issue formal proceedings, effectively putting me on a war footing for court. But first I wanted to know who actually had assets against which I could recover any successful judgement and damages awarded by the court.

The firm conducted some preliminary searches and found that five of the eight had real estate assets, so that gave me confidence that, even relying on those five, I had reasonable grounds to recover the types of damages Partner had first predicted. However, this insight created a noticeable change in the firm's attitude: they immediately dismissed the three defendants who had no property.

This may have been a reasonable consideration from a commercial perspective, but it didn't make those offenders any less culpable. I felt that what we needed was a broader strategy. Who was to say that these three couldn't have paid anyway? After all, there are many forms of assets other than real estate. But despite this argument, my legal team never did develop an alternative strategy, which had very significant consequences as the case progressed.

Statements of claim are like concerns notices, but much more detailed, particularly when it comes to addressing the plaintiff's obligations under defamation law as detailed above. They are also the documents against which any subsequent trial will be assessed, so drafting and serving these correctly is critical.

Not long after drafting the statements of claim, Partner contacted me to discuss a new legal nuance called a *Calderbank offer*. This offer impacts the amount of damages the plaintiff (me) can claim in a statement of claim. Apparently, if I claimed more than what was ultimately awarded in court, costs could be awarded against me, even if I won the case.

Seriously? So now the firm was applying even more pressure to reduce my damages claim. But didn't I have a winning case? Oh, that's right. As Partner had warned me at the beginning, 'There are no guarantees with a court case'.

So again I trimmed a little to protect against this technicality. But this meant that I was now offering a third discount, meaning the collective values were roughly half Partner's initial predicted value, all while my legal costs continued to grow at an alarming rate.

Anyway, out went the statements of claim, which have to be served in person (like in the TV shows where they present papers and say, *you've been served*). This meant using expensive service agents, who always seemed to take two attempts to serve the documents—I assumed because they were paid for each attempt—with no negotiation. But even with the servers' expertise and expense, two of the defendants managed to avoid them, which meant I had to apply to the court for what is called a *substitute service order*, allowing me to serve the defendants via their lawyers, employers, etc, meaning even more costs.

FIRST BARRISTER

Given that this was a significant step towards a formal trial, it was also time to brief a barrister. The firm referred me to First Barrister. Clearly, given the referral, First Barrister wasn't about to put the firm offside, but from what I can gather, First Barrister took one look at the statements of claim sent by First Associate and was appalled. Apparently, they were complete rubbish and, not surprisingly, we started to receive more complaints and objections from the lawyers for the defence about the quality of the statements of claim.

Clearly not wanting to make waves with the firm, First Barrister quietly began redrafting the statement of claim, but it quickly became apparent that this meant even more costs incurred by me because now the very expensive First Barrister was doing the work.

Worse still, the defendants all started to claim 'costs thrown away'. This is a legal entitlement where, if the 'offending' party makes obvious mistakes that create more legal costs for the 'non-offending' party, the non-offending parties can effectively claim the additional costs for dealing with the matter twice. So, in addition to my three discounted values and my ever-growing legal costs, I now owed the defendants money because of the firm's mistakes, all of this before I was close to seeing any recompense from the defendants.

What was going on here? Enough was enough. I told Partner that if he didn't replace First Associate with a far more competent lawyer, I would sack the firm and lodge a complaint with the Law Council. After much back and forth, First Associate was replaced by Second Associate, and between Second Associate and First Barrister, an amended statement of claim was finally served on all eight defendants.

PRE-MEDIATION

By now it was late March 2022, eighteen months after the attacks, and seventeen months after engaging the firm. Only now had they begun to proceed in an effective way, which was critical as we were only eight weeks away from the scheduled mediation session.

Formal mediation is a requirement of most civil court cases, which is a way of trying to settle disputes, if possible, prior to trial. It was also the first time the defendants really started to incur significant legal costs themselves, so Partner and First Barrister assured me that this would increase their incentive to settle.

In fact, this proved to be the case as, after some negotiation, two of the defendants made offers to settle prior to mediation, presumably not to incur legal costs for basically an unwinnable case. This is certainly what I would have done in their shoes. However, the damages offered were considerably less than the third-discount value in their statement of claim, let alone their proportion of Partner's original lofty predictions. Regardless, after much pressure from my legal team, I took a pragmatic approach, concluding that accepting their offers made my remaining case more manageable and provided some much-needed funds with which to continue my legal battle.

What I didn't expect was that, despite my insistence to the contrary, clearly this fourth-discount value sent a signal to my legal team, in particular to First Barrister, that I wanted to settle at any price, which played out in a devastating way at mediation.

Yet again, this settlement also demonstrated my legal team's lack of familiarity with Facebook. Part of the agreement with the settling defendants was that they post an apology on my Facebook business page. Second Associate drafted the agreement without specifying precisely how and where their apology was to be posted. So the defendants created a fake profile, posted the apology as a mention and not a post, and failed to tag me. This ruse meant that virtually none of my friends or clients ever saw the apology, and even if they had, they would not have known who had posted it.

And what was Second Associate's deflating response? 'Well, they've technically done what we asked, so best just move on.' Unbelievable.

MEDIATION

As the mediation approached, it became clear that the two defendants who ducked service wouldn't be attending because they still hadn't submitted the necessary paperwork. By opting out of the mediation, they waived their right to defend themselves, leaving the judge to determine damages based on the evidence we presented. While this ensured default judgment in my favour, it also meant that we would proceed with the trial regardless of the mediation outcome. My legal costs had already exceeded $100,000, with the trial still to come. To my mind, this should have made my legal team more determined to extract maximum damages against the remaining four defendants, three of whom owned real estate, rather than weakening their resolve.

As we had already received documentation outlining the defence of the remaining four defendants attending mediation, we knew that their primary argument was going to be that my reference to Shusha during the war, and my preparation of what they considered Armenian food on the *Russian Influence* show, were extremely provocative actions and justified their response.

Knowing the importance of these issues, many months prior to mediation I had provided my legal team with a briefing document covering the facts of the conflict between Armenia and Azerbaijan, my cooking show, and even my multicultural activities. However, despite this, my legal team steadfastly refused to address any aspect of the mentioned conflict in our prosecution, arguing it was irrelevant to the technicalities of defamation law.

So what was going to be our strategy for the mediation session? Again, alarm bells rang when First Barrister started talking down the severity of one of the defendant's posts. Now remember, I had already limited my actions to only those attackers who had made the most defamatory remarks, as confirmed by the firm right from the outset. And also remember that First Barrister had prepared the amended statement of claim, so why start raising doubt now? But no sensible answer came. It was more just an FYI.

Then, the day before mediation, First Barrister emailed me a ruling of another online defamation case for me to review urgently. After I spent several hours reading through the legalese, I determined that there were very few similarities between my case and the judgement provided in this other case. When I asked First Barrister why he had sent it to me, he replied 'To highlight how difficult it is to win such cases', as the defence actually won that case. I was furious. Why provide this information now, and with such poor context? Clearly my legal team was softening me up for the vendor bashing to come the next day.

Mediation involves all parties coming together at the same time, in person or via Zoom, to see if they can agree on a settlement to avoid the dispute going to trial, all under the supervision and guidance of a qualified mediator.

In my case, given that I was already going to trial for the two defaulting defendants, I didn't feel any urgency to settle, but I went with an open mind.

My husband and I met with Partner and First Barrister for coffee prior to going into the conference facilities to meet the mediator, whom I will call Mediator. The first thing First Barrister shared was that he wasn't confident of our case against another of the defendants coming to mediation. This was now two he had inexplicably raised concerns about, and why so late? But no sensible answer came. It was just another FYI.

Then, in passing, I asked both First Barrister and Partner if they had watched my *Russian Influence* cooking show episode, expecting some light chat or even questions about the food and the map of Azerbaijan. To my amazement, neither had watched the *Russian Influence cooking* show at all. When I asked them why, they both said it was irrelevant to the case, but should it proceed to trial they would watch it then. Such disrespect was hard to believe. From all the hundreds of hours of fees they had charged me, they couldn't find twenty minutes to watch the show that was at the centre of this entire saga.

Still reeling from both these revelations, I followed my legal team into mediation. As the entire mediation session took a total of eight hours, there's no need to relate every conversation, but essentially First Barrister opened up by outlining our case against each of the defendants. They in turn outlined their defence, which included several remarks about me and my businesses that I found insulting, but I held my tongue and waited for Mediator to do his thing. But nothing came. He simply went between the different physical and virtual meeting rooms relaying messages and offers, but never once made any suggestion as to why any party should settle. In other words, he was nothing but a very expensive messenger boy.

By about lunchtime it became apparent that the defendant without property wasn't going to make any reasonable offer. As I considered this defendant to be one of the ringleaders, to my mind this meant that I was definitely going to trial. This should have placed maximum pressure on the remaining three property holders, given that going to trial would cost them many tens of thousands in extra legal fees, whereas for me it was only incremental to the legal fees already incurred.

Clearly, my legal team thought otherwise. As the day ground on, First Barrister became increasing agitated because I wasn't agreeing to the paltry amounts being offered. To stop things coming to a complete halt, I agreed to one settlement, similar to the prior two settlements, again way short of Partner's initial predicted value.

But then the pressure really came from First Barrister. Despite my husband presenting spreadsheets showing I would be left with a significant deficit against the legal fees I had already incurred up to that point, let alone the extra costs of going to trial, First Barrister turned up the heat, insisting I accept the remaining two offers from the property holders.

In the end I caved in, accepting the final two offers, which were even less than the previous settlements, and don't I regret that. It meant that I had settled with five of the eight defendants, including all the property holders, for a cumulative proportionate value of approximately twenty percent of Partner's initial predicted value. How was that, in any way, acting in my best interests? Worse still, I was left tens of thousands of dollars short of the legal fees I had incurred to that point. Did I get any apologies from Partner or First Barrister? Not one.

Going through the mediation process was terrible. On one side I was seeing my trolls' faces and listening to their aggressive lawyers, and on other side I was receiving pressure from my lawyers to accept a settlement that was not in my best interests. It all left me feeling powerless and frustrated. The stress and pain of the whole mediation process took a significant toll on my mental and emotional health.

Now I'm sure that some readers will be wondering why I wasn't firmer with my legal team, or why I accepted the offers I did. Believe me, I have asked myself the same thing many times, which is easy to do in the cold light of retrospect. But let me tell you, this was death by a thousand cuts, inflicted over a very long and emotional period of time, from a team I thought were experts and who were all working in my best interests.

Clearly this wasn't the case. In fact, I've concluded that they were simply working to meet their own legal fees, and not to achieve any meaningful compensation for the harm and hurt I had incurred. I will carry the cost of that misrepresentation and attitude for the rest of my days. For now, all I can hope is that my experience can help others to be more vigilant and forthright should they ever find themselves in the same position.

And now what about the remaining three defendants?

BEFORE THE TRIAL

Making the decision to take the remaining three defendants to trial was excruciating for me. I knew it was a risky move, because even if I won, there was a chance that I would never receive any compensation from them. However, considering the severity of their attacks, I couldn't let them get away without facing the consequences. It was a difficult and emotional decision to make, but ultimately I knew I had to stand up for myself and continue to fight for justice.

Mediation ended in late June 2022 and the trial was scheduled for early November 2022, which meant I had already endured a gruelling twenty months of stress and trauma, and the thought of facing a trial only added to that burden.

Given this, after consulting with my legal team, who confirmed that we had ample time to prepare for trial, Graeme and I decided to take advantage of the lifting Covid travel restrictions and visit my family in Baku, whom I had not seen in three years. We then went on to tour England and Scotland, allowing me to take a much-needed break from the legal battle. This trip took up most of September, which was a wonderful experience, and was relatively uneventful from a legal perspective.

Upon returning in early October, roughly one month before trial, I was immediately contacted by my legal team, who asked me to urgently prepare witness affidavits, mostly to support my 'publication' proof, but also so the witnesses could prepare for their own appearance in court.

Imagine the surprise my friends and clients expressed when, out of the blue, I contacted them and asked them to sign affidavits confirming that they had seen the offending posts almost two years earlier, and told them they would be appearing in court in a few weeks' time. Most had commented against the posts at the time, so documented proof wasn't the main issue, but being asked with such little notice to be a witness and having to sign an affidavit was problematic. Not surprisingly, I had some pushback, which strained some friendships. Mostly, the witnesses were understandably concerned about the possibility of being targeted by the same people who had attacked me once it became known that they were supporting my case.

A pretrial hearing is a meeting with the presiding judge, where any last-minute questions or formalities can be addressed before the trial begins. To address my witnesses' concerns, I asked First Barrister to request that our witnesses remain anonymous, or to have their identities disguised to prevent the possibility of them being trolled. I knew this request went against legal principles, but it was a major concern for our witnesses, and I wanted to see how First Barrister would handle it, particularly given his performance during the mediation.

Unfortunately, I got what I expected. First Barrister didn't even seem to grasp the witnesses' concerns and instead suggested hiding their physical addresses. Moreover, he appeared more concerned with protecting his standing with the judge than mounting a plausible argument to protect my witnesses. Unsurprisingly, the judge denied our request, and that was the last straw for me.

I immediately dismissed First Barrister, even though we had less than two weeks to find a replacement in time for the trial. As for my lawyers, they never did explain why they waited so long to arrange my witnesses, leaving them so little time to seek legal advice, let alone block out time to appear at the trial if required. This request could have been made months earlier, immediately after mediation, and well before we went on holiday. This was even more evidence that they were at best disorganised, at worst incompetent.

Fortunately, I secured the services of a more junior barrister, whom I will call Second Barrister, who turned out to be much more competent, and quickly understood the details of my case and proved to be a valuable asset during the trial.

This whole pretrial period was undoubtedly the most challenging time of the entire process. Graeme and I worked full time helping the legal team and witnesses prepare for trial. The stress and pressure of the intense preparation, coupled with the financial pressure, had a continuing detrimental effect on my health and I was exhausted even before the trial commenced.

THE TRIAL

It's hard for me to speak in detail about the trial because this was my first time in a courtroom, so I have nothing to compare it with. Suffice to say it was nothing like in the movies: quite the opposite, in fact. It was incredibly tedious, taking three days when it should have taken one. In large part this was to accommodate the one appearing defendant, who was self-represented, and for whom the judge went to great lengths to ensure they properly understood the proceedings, the law, and their obligations and opportunities.

I never imagined the court would be so accommodating, but that doesn't mean I would recommend self-representation, because, despite the judge's assistance, the defendant was clearly out of their depth and in my opinion did little to help their defence.

Fortunately, in the end, all the witness affidavits were accepted into evidence without challenge, and only two people were asked to appear in person by Second Barrister, but this still caused me enormous frustration and embarrassment at having wasted the time of so many people.

As explained earlier, one of my main frustrations with my legal team was their gagging of the core issue around Nagorno-Karabakh. Now, I understand their arguments for doing this, but this frustration was compounded when, right on cue, the defendant spent much of their opening and closing addresses talking specifically about Nagorno-Karabakh. The gagging approach meant we had little formal evidence to counter even their most blatantly false claims. For instance, the defendant stated that I was a liar because I said Karabakh is Azerbaijan. Even having a standard map of Azerbaijan as part of our evidence would have allowed us to immediately discredit this.

In any case, my strong advice for anyone in this situation is to insist that your lawyers give you a chance to be heard, regardless of the specific relevance to the law. You will feel much better for it. For this reason, I was actually most comfortable in the witness box, even when being cross-examined, because finally this was my time to be heard.

Also, regardless of the electronic age, and how the legal system purports to have embraced it, all submission documents should be in bound hard copy. My husband, who sat with me throughout, had done this in advance for the eight hundred pages tendered, and it was a lifesaver on several occasions when the court and my legal team were struggling to accurately refer to the correct documents.

By the end of the trial I thought Second Barrister had done a good job presenting our case and that the defendant had submitted nothing to explain or exonerate their guilt. Therefore I was surprised when the judge reserved her judgement, meaning we would have to reconvene again at a later date to hear her findings.

THE DECISION

After enduring another agonising four-month wait, we returned to court to hear the judge's decision. In late March 2023, nearly two and a half years since the attacks began, the judge delivered a short summary of her full judgment, affirming all defendants guilty of defamation across all the imputations we raised. This included her determination that all posts had been published to a considerable audience and that the defendants had acted with malice, causing significant hurt and harm to me.

This verdict brought a mix of emotions. On one hand, it provided the long-awaited validation that I had been defamed in a serious and malicious manner. This confirmation served as a vindication, reaffirming that the harm inflicted upon me was not trivial but substantial, and deserving of legal recognition.

However, alongside this validation came a bitter realisation. The judgment offered no clarity on why my legal team had pushed for settlement during mediation, advocating for significantly reduced compensation from the first four defendants. Yet, even more disheartening was the realisation that the battle was far from over.

Now, the burden falls upon me, rather than the courts, to secure the awarded damages from the defendants. Despite hoping they would accept responsibility and honour the court's decision; they have shown no inclination to do so.

As of now, all three remaining defendants persist in disregarding my requests for restitution, further extending the process and increasing my legal expenses. Compounding these delays is the 'privacy' protection they are willingly afforded by their employers and social services, despite knowing of their convictions and them blatantly flouting the directions of the courts. It is frustrating to realise that after enduring immense stress, financial strain, and time committed, I am no closer to covering my legal costs or receiving compensation for the harm caused, whilst they hide behind protections that should not apply to such individuals.

Despite my disappointment and frustration, I remain determined to pursue justice and hold the defendants accountable for their actions. While the legal process has been arduous and costly, I refuse to let their misconduct go unchecked. Until now, I have acted with dignity, consideration, and respect, refraining from naming and shaming these individuals on social media and in general media. But if they persist in their refusal to comply with court orders, I may have no choice but to take a different approach, including revealing their identities. Though the road ahead may be challenging, I will continue to fight for what is right.

Facing my offenders in court and mediation brought up a range of emotions, including fear, anxiety, anger, and sadness. It was hard to confront those who had caused harm to me, and to relive the trauma of the incidents. However, while it has been a long and challenging road, I am proud that I stood up to these bullies. In doing so, I have also learned a lot about myself and my resilience in the face of adversity, and I am stronger and wiser for the experience, albeit financially ruined.

CONCLUSION

Drawing from my personal experiences, other victims of online abuse often seek my advice on the question, "Should I pursue legal action against cyber bullies?" This is a deeply personal choice, and each circumstance is unique, primarily governed by your ability to simply ignore the attack. There is no shame in not taking legal action, because for many people this will ultimately be the least stressful and least expensive decision.

Regardless, assuming your priority is to minimise the personal and professional impact of the trolling, it's crucial to carefully follow these steps, before ultimately deciding on legal action:

- **Firstly, consult the guidance in Appendix I:**
  - Collect all evidence related to the cyberbullying incident.
  - Demand that the perpetrators remove the offensive content.

- **Next, promptly report the abuse to the online service or platform:**
  - Again refer to the guidance in Appendix I
  - As the reporting mechanisms for each platform are changing all the time, you should also search online for additional assistance and guidance.

- **If the first two steps prove unsuccessful:**
  - Involve regulatory authorities to assist in addressing the issue with the service, platforms, or even the perpetrators. For example, the Australian eSafety Commissioner's website[6] indicates they have powers to assist in serious cases.

    "In the most serious cases, when the service or platform does not help, eSafety can direct them to remove harmful content that has been sent to an Australian, or posted or shared about them. Sometimes, we may be able to fine or take legal action against a service or platform that refuses to remove harmful content, or the person who sent, posted or shared it."

- **Consider engaging the police and law enforcement:**
  - Explore relevant criminal codes, such as racial vilification, for additional avenues of resolution.

- **Lastly, remember:**
  - The legal process may amplify, not alleviate, existing emotional distress from the attack.
  - Suing for defamation is not a quick or guaranteed route to substantial damages compared to the legal fees you will incur.
  - Despite its intimidatory grandeur, lengthy complex processes, and exorbitant costs, the legal system remains largely ineffective in forcing perpetrators to pay the awarded damages and costs.

---

[6]   https://www.esafety.gov.au/

If, after all these considerations, you still opt for legal action:

- Good for you.
- Choose your lawyer carefully. Make sure they understand technology, social media, and online defamation.
- Ensure their grasp aligns with the guidance in Appendix I of this book.
- Hold them accountable throughout the process, question anything you don't understand, challenge anything you don't agree with, and don't hesitate to change legal representation if needed.

6. THE TRUE COST AND IMPACT

Over the past two and a half years, many well-meaning friends and colleagues have questioned my reasons for pursuing legal action, inferring that this whole situation was nothing but a bit of a storm in a teacup.

Unfortunately, the reality was far from that, as these attacks had a deep impact on my health, my businesses, and my relationships with those closest to me. I understand that sharing these details may please my attackers, but I believe it's important to shed light on the profound and lasting devastation that online trolling can cause its victims.

MY HEALTH

In the previous chapter, I covered the financial stress I incurred from pursuing legal justice. While that has been significant, the toll on my physical and mental wellbeing has been immeasurable. Prior to the attacks, I was a passionate and driven entrepreneur who enjoyed nothing more than entertaining friends and clients in my home. I would often go above and beyond, spending hours chatting with clients about topics far beyond my products and services. While this was exhausting, it reflected my unwavering dedication to providing exceptional customer service and engagement.

Initially, when the online attack occurred I was overwhelmed with shock. It was hard to believe that even one person, let alone fifty people, who had no personal connection with me, could write such despicable things about me. It was like a dagger in my heart when some of the attackers lied about my customer service and spewed racially motivated hatred. But worst were the threats of violence, which left me scared and stunned with disbelief.

From the moment the first posts hit my Facebook pages, my obsession with trying to stop them grew. I tried everything I could to end it quickly, from reaching out to Facebook to seeking help from the authorities. But as hope of a quick resolution faded, my anxiety about the attacks' longevity increased. As my job requires me to be active on social media, this was a constant source of anxiety and discomfort during the legal proceedings, knowing that my every move was being monitored by my attackers and their lawyers. Just taking my phone in my hands or turning on my computer made me feel stressed.

The compound effect of this daily struggle was profound, and I regularly woke up exhausted and depressed from the nightmares I experienced at night.

In an attempt to manage the nightmares and anxiety, I sought the help of two psychiatrists and two psychologists. They confirmed my condition and prescribed antidepressants, but unfortunately the medication had severe side effects, which forced me to discontinue taking it after only a few months. I found some temporary relief through traditional Chinese treatments such as acupuncture, massage and herbal medication, but the high cost of these treatments made them unsustainable for me due to my financial situation and the significant legal expenses I was incurring.

Physically, I no longer felt safe in my own home or in public spaces. I had to stop conducting beauty consultations at home, which were most effective when done in person, and I could only consult with clients online. As a result, my earnings took a significant hit at a time when I could least afford it, due to my mounting legal costs. The constant fear of being attacked or criticised weighed heavily on me, and I declined many social events and friendly catch-ups to avoid being asked about the attack, or about my chocolate business.

In turn, I became so afraid that I couldn't leave the house on my own for many months. My husband had to be with me all the time, which affected his job. To add to that, we had to install security cameras around our property, something I never thought we would need. In every aspect of my social life I felt like I was being watched, and even taking a holiday seemed wrong. Even when my husband and I had visited my family overseas, I was too afraid to mention it online, worried that someone would attack my home while I was away.

My sense of social isolation only increased as I withdrew further. I rarely experienced positive emotions and often felt utterly helpless.

Even now, the memory of those vile comments can still bring me to tears and make me shake. The effects of online trolling are long-lasting, and the toll it takes on one's physical and mental wellbeing cannot be underestimated. In my case, the online trolling had manifested into real physical harm for me. So let me tell you, this saga was far from a storm in a teacup.

MY BUSINESSES

Additionally, the trolling has had a long-term negative effect on my businesses, especially since they all require me to be active on social media. The biggest hit has been on my Enjoy Dark Chocolate business, which was my first business venture and my 'baby'. It brought me great joy to create new chocolates and share them with my friends and family. However, for the past two and a half years that has brought only hurt and frustration; I've had to repeatedly disappoint my loyal customers by saying that I don't have any chocolates to sell, and explain why.

The trolling attack could not have come at a worse time for my Enjoy Dark Chocolate business. With the Covid-19 lockdowns ending in late October 2020, I was fortunate enough to secure the services of my chocolatiers again, who had been struggling to make ends meet themselves during the lockdown. But just as the first production run commenced, and my Christmas marketing campaign was about to launch, the trolling attack began.

Confused, I decided to halt production while I dealt with the attacks and the effect they were having on me. Unfortunately, because I was not able to provide a firm recommencement date, my staff found alternative work. This meant that restarting my chocolate production required me to find new, equally talented staff, as well as deal with the reputational damage from the trolls. Unfortunately, all subsequent attempts to secure alternative chocolatier staff, ranging from simply advertising for casual staff to negotiating outsourcing arrangements with established chocolate businesses, came to naught. Every time I tried and failed to re-establish the business, it reminded me of the senseless reasons why I was in that situation, and I suffered further frustration and depression as a result.

Even though most of the fake reviews on both my Enjoy Dark Chocolate and Khuraman Armstrong Facebook pages have now been removed, I assume because the offenders learned of my legal action, the reviews were up for a very long time and have permanently devalued my previous 5-star rating on both pages.

All of this has resulted in a significant loss of income for me, compounded further by the constant financial costs and pressure from the legal proceedings and medical costs. It has wiped out our savings towards the purchase of our own home, meaning that dream is also increasingly unlikely, which further impacts my mental outlook. And with no guarantee of financial redress from the remaining defendants, our financial outlook is a continuing source of stress and sadness.

MY RELATIONSHIPS

I am eternally grateful for the support of my friends and clients during this time, and their efforts to counteract the negative reviews and comments on Facebook. However, as time has passed, understandably their attention has turned back to their own lives, leaving me feeling isolated and alone.

I have also experienced some deeply humiliating situations in which people, who were aware of my legal proceedings, have wrongly assumed that I hold prejudice towards Armenians. One particular incident occurred when

I declined an invitation to a Zoom lecture without knowing the nationality of the lecturer. I soon learned of gossip suggesting that I refused to attend because the lecturer was Armenian. This accusation was entirely false and hurtful. I have never judged anyone based on their race, and such rumours only serve to perpetuate unfair stereotypes and misconceptions.

To make matters worse, I have even received screenshots from members of the Russian Women's group featuring comments or articles about Armenians, seemingly waiting to see if I will respond negatively. This kind of behaviour is incredibly triggering for me, as it insinuates that I share the same hatred of others that has been directed towards me. As a result, I find myself increasingly withdrawing from social media and individual conversations in order to avoid similar discussions or comments.

Our marriage has also suffered because of the attacks, although fortunately our love has remained strong. Before the attacks, Graeme and I spent countless hours together, even during the Covid-19 lockdowns, working hard on growing our businesses, and planning for our next trips overseas and buying our dream home. These were important goals for us, and we were happy to put other pleasures on hold in order to save money and make them a reality.

However, since the legal proceedings started, our relationship has been put under immense pressure. Given his experience as a senior business executive, Graeme agreed to take the lead in communicating with our lawyers so I wouldn't have to deal with the persistent stress. But it has been a challenge for him to strike the right balance between keeping me informed and shielding me from the mundane requirements of the proceedings, causing Graeme his own share of stress and anxiety. It's taken up hundreds of hours of his time and attention, which in turn has affected his own work arrangements.

FRIENDLY ADVICE

As mentioned, I've also received a lot of friendly advice over the past two years, ranging from 'Just ignore them' to 'Change your contact details' or 'Cut your losses and let it go'.

However, these responses only serve to empower and embolden trolls. Therefore, I urge every reader of this book to consider what you would do in my position. If we do not stop this behaviour now, it will continue to escalate. It requires us all to be strong and put this issue above our own self-interests.

For example, the executive producer of the *Russian Influence* show, who also experienced trolling on her YouTube channel, took a very a cynical attitude towards her offenders. When I questioned her about why she didn't take action against them, she responded cheerfully, saying, 'Any anti-advertisement is advertisement for me,' and 'Even the haters will watch this show now.'

Worse still, while she initially appeared supportive of my decision to take legal action against the trolls, after I requested a simple affidavit from her to confirm that she had featured me in her cooking show, she continuously delayed providing it until, on the very last day, she cited her husband's consultation with his corporate lawyer as a reason why she could not sign the document.

Likewise, the administrator of the Facebook group where the trolling originated also seemed supportive initially. However, when it came time to provide a straightforward affidavit to the court confirming her role as the group's administrator, she suddenly refused, citing her husband's strong opposition to her getting involved. It is unfortunate when women who present themselves as strong and independent then use their husbands as shields or excuses for their own actions or inactions.

There were even other Facebook users who, having witnessed my trolling, reached out to me, sharing that they had also previously been bullied by the same offenders who attacked me. They expressed their support for me and were pleased to see someone standing up against the perpetrators. However, when I asked if they would be willing to join me and provide a statement to the court, they became uneasy and scared. While I respect their feelings and decisions, it's important to remember that standing up against bullying requires a collective effort. The more people who speak up and act, the greater the chances of effecting change.

And to help everyone feel safer online, I urge you to write to your federal politicians and demand that they hold social media companies accountable for any hurtful and defamatory content that is published on their platforms.

And please, before you post anything online that could potentially hurt someone else, take a moment to consider the impact of your words. Put yourself in their shoes. Would you still feel entitled to speak out so strongly if the same thing were done to you or your loved ones?

FROM VICTIM TO VICTOR

I started writing this book immediately after the court case, thinking I would complete it while everything was fresh in my mind. However, I was also in a place of victimhood and hurt, so even though I knew it was an important undertaking, reliving the events of the previous two and a half years was a constant source of stress for me. The fact that the judge was taking so long to give her judgment also didn't help. Eventually I had to put my writing on hold. I didn't know for how long, but I knew I needed to take control of my own life before I could begin to help others.

Then I heard that Dr Joe Dispensa, a famous lecturer on neuroscience and quantum physics, was coming to Australia for a week-long retreat in March 2023. I knew immediately that I wanted to join the retreat, believing it would help with my recovery, but I didn't know just how profound an effect it would have on my life.

Within minutes of the tickets going on sale in December 2022, I bought my ticket and waited impatiently for the event, hoping that some kind of magic would occur. As I explained earlier, I hit my darkest days immediately after the court hearing. I was depleted physically, mentally and financially, and exhausted from working to pay my legal fees. Even the mention of the court case, or a call from my lawyers, would send me into deep depression. I kept telling my husband that I didn't want to live. I was scared by my feelings and thoughts.

As the date of the event approached, I felt a little more optimistic. I completed Dr Joe's online courses and concentrated fully on improving my physical health.

In one of the online courses I was asked to think about certain events, and the feelings I experienced when those events had occurred. Then I was asked to pick one word that I associated with addressing those feelings. I chose *resolution*, which to me represented the words freedom, safe, healed, creative, inspirational, justice, being unlimited, and getting justice against those who had hurt me. I needed resolution so I could move on to the next chapter of my life.

My actual healing journey started at the event in March 2023. It wasn't easy, as I was still too focused on my problems. And of course, there was no magic solution. Healing requires a commitment and a willingness to change. I had to break the 'habit of being myself' and reinvent a new self.

Soon my goals and wishes quickly moved far beyond the problems I brought to the event. While resolution was still high on my list, I discovered much more for myself. I finally felt joy again after my first walking meditation on the beach with a thousand other people, such a simple yet powerful experience. I knew then that my healing had begun.

After meditating on resolution several times, towards the end of the event I received a phone call from my husband advising me that two days after my return from the retreat, the judge would deliver her findings in court. Hallelujah! I was so relieved to know the verdict was in, even though I was still nervous about the outcome.

A week later I had my successful judgement. That was when I realised that regardless of the amount of damages awarded, or when I would see any money from the perpetrators, I was a *victor*. I had done all I could. I had stood up for myself. I did everything I could to hold people accountable so they wouldn't hurt others. And now it was time to release and move on. Perhaps not surprisingly, since the event I haven't missed a day of meditation.

In a further sign of resolution, around the time of releasing this book, I managed to hire new qualified chocolatier staff and Enjoy Dark Chocolate production has cautiously recommenced while I reconnect with my previous clients and nervously post my first chocolate promotions since the attacks.

It hasn't been an easy journey, and there is no quick fix or magic pill when it comes to healing. I've had my fair share of setbacks since my return from the retreat, and although I still experience night terrors, I haven't let that discourage me. Despite these challenges, I feel much stronger and more empowered than ever before. It's as if I've been given a new lease on life. I now have the energy and motivation to share my story through this book, which will hopefully make a difference to the lives of many others who are also experiencing online harassment, bullying or defamation.

It is also my sincere hope that we can quickly move past this era of online lawlessness, and implement cyber protections that are equivalent to, or better than, those we enjoy in the physical world. In closing, I hope you've found this book, including its appendices, helpful and informative. Thanks for reading.

Khuraman Armstrong

APPENDIX I. THE FIRST TWENTY-FOUR HOURS

DEFINITIONS

Although the content and advice provided in this guide can be applicable to other social media and review platforms, as of the time of writing the specific terms used and guidance provided are limited to Facebook only.

It's crucial to understand that the available options and actions for someone experiencing a trolling or bullying attack on Facebook can vary considerably, depending on the type of Facebook page or publication. Therefore, it's important to comprehend the subtle differences between them, as outlined in the following definitions.

Fortunately I had a reasonable understanding of these variations at the time of my attack. Nonetheless, I still made simple mistakes that significantly lengthened and potentially jeopardised my subsequent legal battle. This chapter aims to assist you in avoiding similar mistakes when navigating the emotionally charged first few days of an attack.

YOU

In this guide I refer to you in the context of a reader who is potentially the subject of an online attack.

PROFILE PAGES

A *profile page* is the default page everyone gets when they create a Facebook account, and it represents *you as an individual*. Among its many other features, a profile page allows you to connect with family members and friends who are also users of Facebook, in addition to uploading photos, and creating posts and stories.

BUSINESS PAGES

Business pages, which you create from your profile page, support a business interest or brand. Business pages allow you to connect with customers or other business associates, post updates about your products or services, and collect reviews.

GROUP PAGES

Group pages are another type of page created from a profile page, and they are used for communicating shared interests with specific people. You can create a group for anything, such as a family reunion, after-work sports team, or book club, and also customise each group's privacy settings based on who you want to join and see the group:

- Public: Anyone on Facebook can join the group and see who is in it and what they post.
- Private: Only those members approved by administrators can join and see who's in the group and what they post.

When joining someone else's group on Facebook, keep in mind that unless you are an administrator of that group, you cannot directly control or remove negative posts or comments made against you. Only group administrators can take any of the steps outlined in this guide.

PUBLICATIONS

Publications refer to various types of uploads, contributions or remarks that can be made on the Facebook platform. There are two main groups of publications:

- original publications, which include personal posts, third-party posts and reviews; and
- secondary publications, which include comments and emojis added to original publications or other secondary comments.

When I use the term publications, I'm referring to all the different types collectively; however, when I'm discussing a particular type of publication, I will specify it by name.

PERSONAL POSTS

Personal posts refer to any original content created and shared by you on Facebook. Typically, personal posts will appear on your profile or business page, but they can also be shared within Facebook groups. These posts can be set to be visible to the public, or visible to friends and close friends only.

While it is possible to delete personal posts on your own pages or in group pages, doing so will also remove all comments and reactions associated with that post. It's important to note that deleting posts can also eliminate potential evidence in the case of a trolling attack, so it's not recommended as an immediate reaction. Further guidance on how to handle trolling attacks can be found in this guide.

THIRD-PARTY POSTS

Third-party posts refer to the original publications created by someone else on their Facebook pages, or within a Facebook group. These usually consist of posts or stories where you may or may not be tagged, and they will remain on the third party's Facebook pages. You cannot hide or delete third-party posts, regardless of the type of page they are published on. Only the third party themselves or a group administrator can remove them.

REVIEWS

Reviews serve the same purpose on Facebook as on other review platforms, allowing customers to provide honest feedback about businesses from whom they have purchased, for the benefit of new potential customers. These reviews are created by third-party individuals and appear on the business page but not on profile pages. Unfortunately, it's not possible for page owners to delete Facebook reviews, which makes them a popular tool for trolling attacks against businesses and brands.

Only the individual who wrote the review or Facebook's team can remove a review. Page owners can flag a review to notify Facebook's team to remove it, but if the review has at least one comment on it, this won't be possible. Once a review is reported, Facebook will evaluate it to determine whether it violates their policies. If so, it should be removed; however, there is no guarantee that fake reviews will be removed since Facebook is a flawed system.

If these fake reviews continue to harm your business, you can disable reviews on your page. However, this may weaken your online reputation, and your ability to attract and convert customers on Facebook.

COMMENTS

Comments are a type of secondary publication that can be added to an original personal post, third-party post, review, or another secondary comment. They can be added by anyone who can access the original publication, and are often used as a means of online attack, regardless of the content of the original publication. Deleting comments is only possible on your profile page, but you can hide individual comments under any personal post on your own profile page or business pages. This is a crucial option that is explored further in this guide.

EMOJIS

Emojis are a form of secondary publication that convey a contributor's thoughts on any original publication or secondary comment through graphical expressions. Like comments, anyone who can access the original publication or secondary comments can add emojis. The rules that apply to the original publication type dictate your ability to hide or remove emojis.

Although emojis themselves are unlikely to be the cause of an online attack, they are essential when it comes to some technical aspects of defamation law, which I have explained in the chapter titled **My Legal Journey**. They should not be disregarded as potential evidence for any future events.

CONTRIBUTORS

Contributors are third-party Facebook users who post an original or secondary publication that references you or your business or brand.

OFFENDERS

Offenders are the individuals who participate in online attacks by publishing threatening or defamatory posts, reviews or comments.

ATTACK

Attack includes all forms of online trolling, bullying and defamation by an individual or group of individuals.

KEY ACTIONS

The purpose of this guide is to provide instructions on how to capture evidence of an online attack on Facebook. While it focuses on the *how* aspect, it's also important to understand the *why* behind the process. For this, I recommend you read the chapter titled **My Legal Journey**.

Capturing and cataloguing screenshots is a crucial aspect of your response to an online attack on Facebook, as outlined in the following steps. Although it may seem repetitive and time-consuming, the more comprehensive your screenshots and cataloguing, the smoother the process will be when working with authorities or your legal team as they:

- Assess the removal of any offending posts or reviews
- Properly advise you of your legal options
- Maximise your chances of prosecuting offenders in a court of law

I recommend that you perform the following steps on a PC or laptop rather than a smartphone because the larger screen size allows for the capture of greater detail in a single screenshot, and it's also easier to correctly title and organise screenshot images as you take them. However, if you don't have access to a PC or laptop, using a smartphone is still better than not capturing any evidence at all. In such cases, make supplementary notes to help reconcile the default image file name with the cataloguing recommended in the following steps.

To minimise the number of screenshots needed, hide any Facebook slide-out menus if possible, and 'zoom out' the browser view while ensuring that the screenshots remain legible. Additionally, adjust the size of your browser window so that each screenshot captures the following information:

- Page title and URL at the top
- Date and time displayed in the task bar
- As much of the thread as optimal

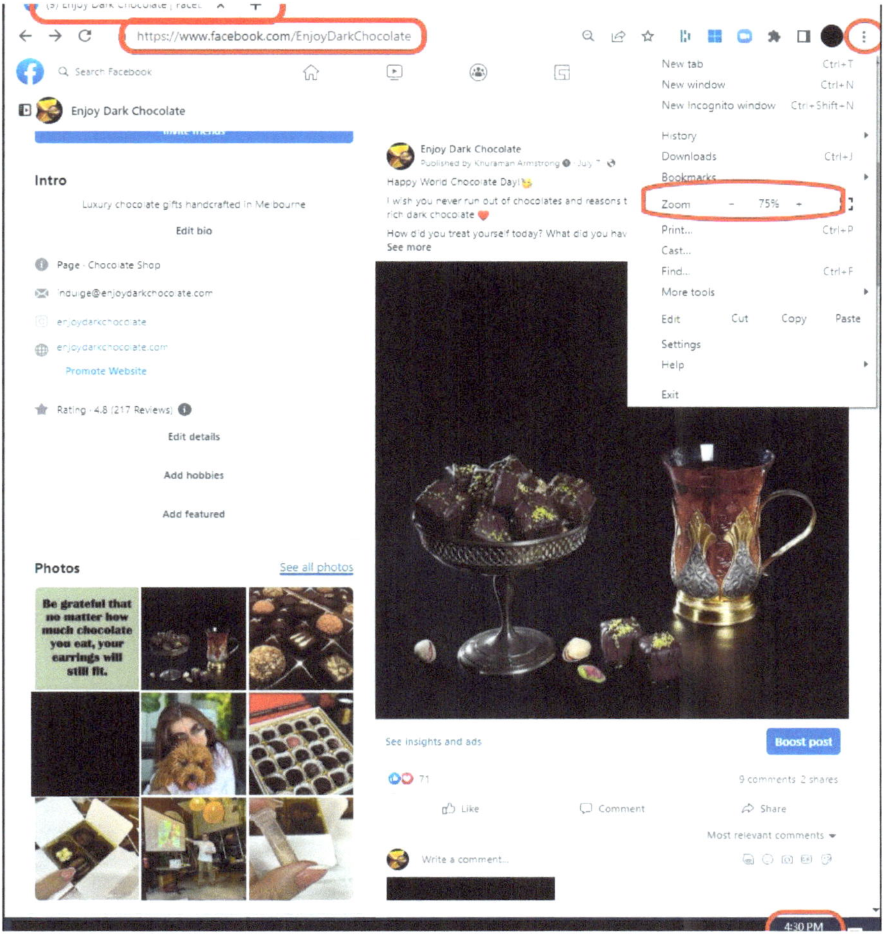

STEP 1. HALT FURTHER ATTACKS

BLOCK PROFILES

Blocking the attacker's Facebook profile is a quick and easy way to stop them from making further posts. In addition, temporarily blocking the profiles instead of deleting them will give you time to perform these steps and to secure proof. Blocking can be done on both personal and business pages by going to the profile of the offender and clicking on the 3-dot icon (...) on the bottom right of the cover photo, and then selecting Block. Alternatively, you can access the blocking feature from the settings & privacy option in the menu of your own page by clicking Settings & Privacy, Settings, Blocking, Block User, and then selecting the profile you wish to block.

TURN OFF COMMENTS

If you find yourself facing a group attack similar to what I experienced, you may want to consider limiting or turning off comments on the original publication to control who can add new comments or contribute to another post, comment or review. This can be done on both profile and business pages, and can be reversed at a later time.

To change the comment settings for an individual public post on your page, first navigate to the post and then follow these steps:

- Click the 3-dot icon (...) in the top right of the post.
- Click Who Can Comment on Your Post?
- Choose who is allowed to comment on your public post:

1. Public
2. Friends
3. Profiles and pages you mention

Anyone who is not in your selected comment audience will not see the comment box below the post, but they will be able to see that you have restricted who can comment.

TURN OFF REVIEWS

As I have explained throughout the book, fake reviews are one of the most damaging tools used by trolls, because you can't remove them. Therefore you should temporarily turn off reviews on your Business page until you are confident the attack has passed. This will hide the Reviews tab but your existing reviews will still be there for when you turn Reviews back on again.

- Click your Page's profile photo in the top right.
- Click Settings and Privacy in the dropdown menu, then click Settings.
- Click Privacy in the left menu, then click Page and tagging.
- Toggle 'Allow others to view and leave reviews on your Page?' to on or off

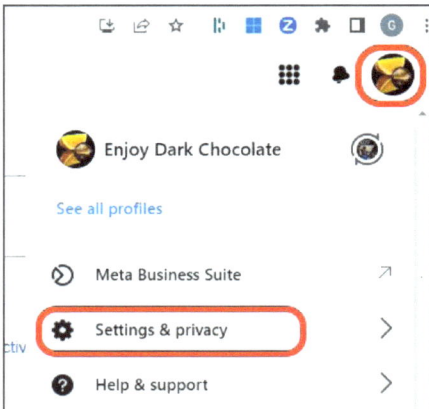

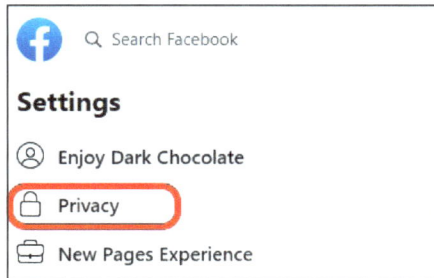

STEP 2. SET UP A CATALOGUE STRUCTURE

These folder structures and naming conventions may seem complex, but taking a minute to create them will keep your screenshots organised and easy to reference, even if you have multiple offenders to track. Failing to do so can cause unnecessary stress and confusion later on. To capture the details of each offender, create a folder titled with their profile name. For example:

- MarySmith

For capturing details of each of your Facebook pages, including insights, ratings and full thread images, create a folder titled with the page name and type. For example:

- KhuramanArmstrongPersonalPage
- KhuramanArmstrongBusinessPage
- EnjoyDarkChocolateBusinessPage

With your folder structure in place, you can begin taking screenshots of the offending publications.

STEP 3. START SCREENSHOTTING

SCREENSHOTTING PAGE INSIGHTS

To begin, take a screenshot of your page's overall statistics for each affected page. To do this, click on Insights in the left-hand slide-out menu, and then click on each of the *Home, Your Page,* and *Audience* sub-menus.

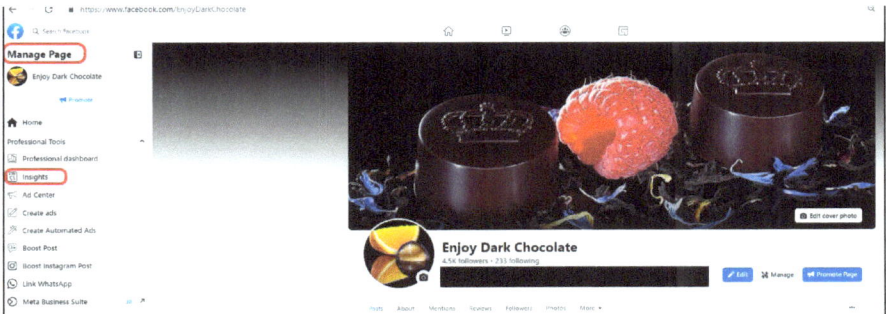

Save the images in the appropriate page folder and title them with the page details and statistic type. For example:

- EnjoyDarkChocolateBusinessPage—Analytics20221207-Home

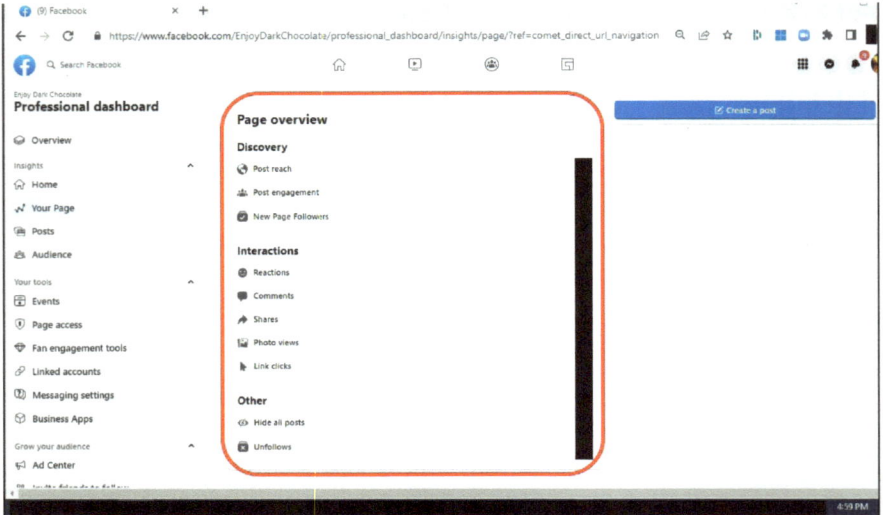

- EnjoyDarkChocolateBusinessPage—Analytics20221207-YourPage

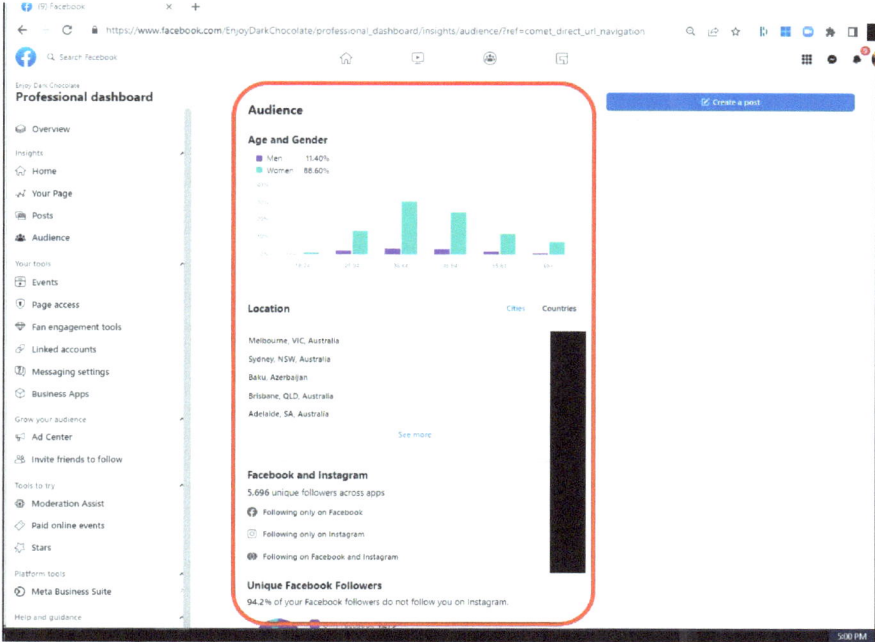

- EnjoyDarkChocolateBusinessPage—Analytics20221207-Audience

As part of documenting any fake reviews on your business page, it's important to take frequent screenshots of the rating score and review count. These screenshots should be named and dated appropriately for easy reference later.

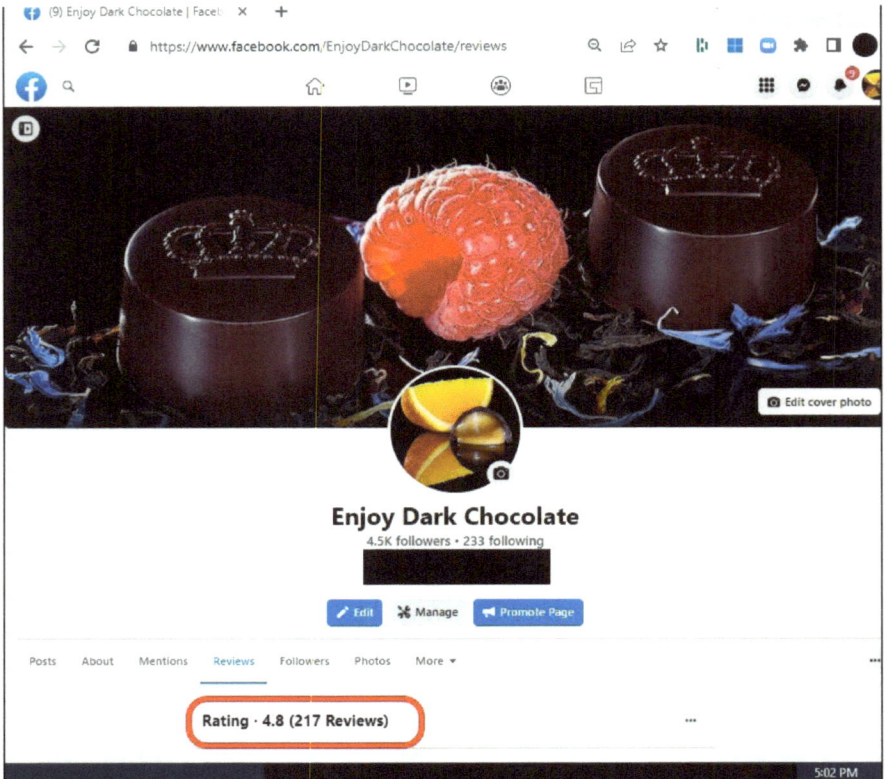

- EnjoyDarkChocolateBusinessPage—Rating20221207

SCREENSHOTTING FULL THREADS

Capturing screenshots of threads and individual posts is a tedious but critical part of the process, which may need to be repeated several times. This is essential to prove the context and chronology of events surrounding the attack and your attackers and can be crucial evidence in a court case.

I recommend beginning with capturing the full-thread images as they may provide significant context and evidence. To do this, go to the original post or review and select *All Comments* under the comments filter option. Then expand the original post's text at the top, and every comment and sub-comment thread within the publication, ensuring that every piece of text in the entire thread is visible. Additionally, adjust the size of your browser window so that for each screenshot you can see the page title and URL at the top, the time shown in the task bar, and as much of the thread as possible. Finally, working from the top of the post down, take screenshots of the entire post or review, making sure to include every comment and sub-comment as you capture the entire thread.

Save each screenshot image in the appropriate page folder, and title individual images with the same naming convention as the folder, plus the thread details and a unique *-PartNumber* ID for each image, defining the order of the screenshots, starting with the originating post or review as *Part1*. For example:

- EnjoyDarkChocolateBusinessPage-MyHappyWorldChocolateDayPost-20201007-Part1

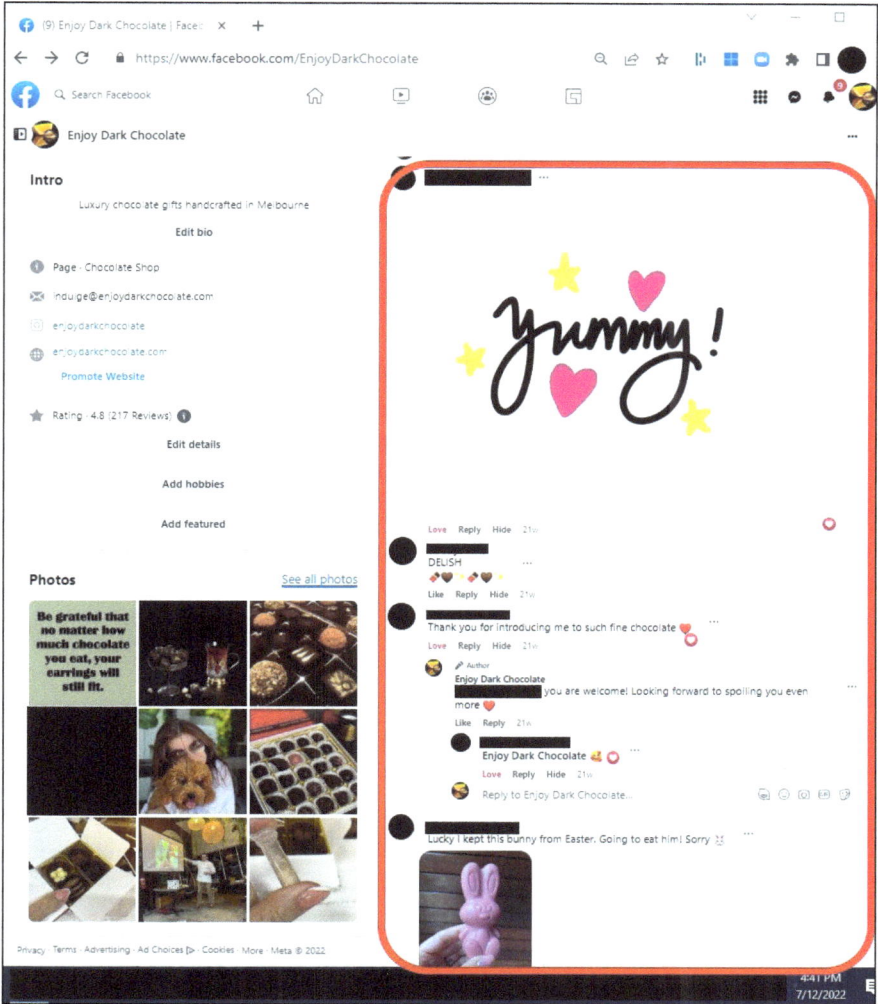

- EnjoyDarkChocolateBusinessPage-MyHappyWorldChocolateDayPost-20201007-Part2

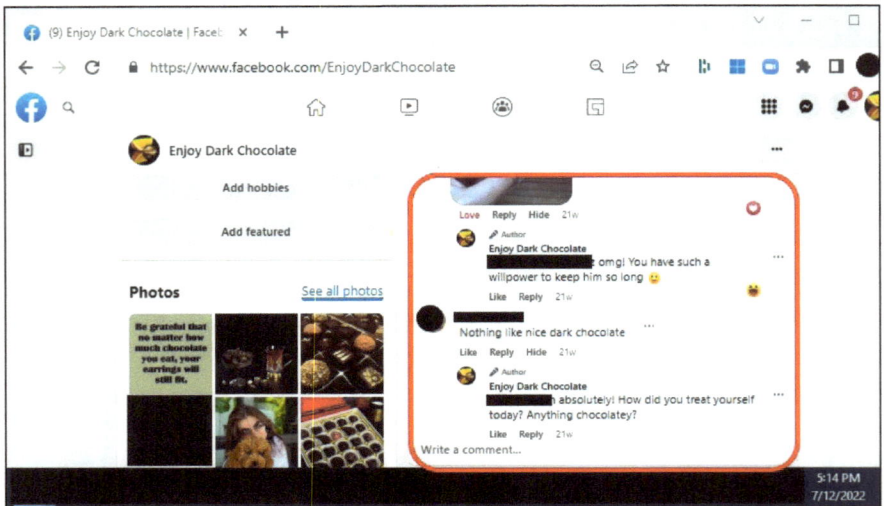

- EnjoyDarkChocolateBusinessPage-MyHappyWorldChocolateDayPost-20201007-Part3

SCREENSHOTTING POST INSIGHTS

Immediately below most personal posts you will see a link to See Insights and Ads.

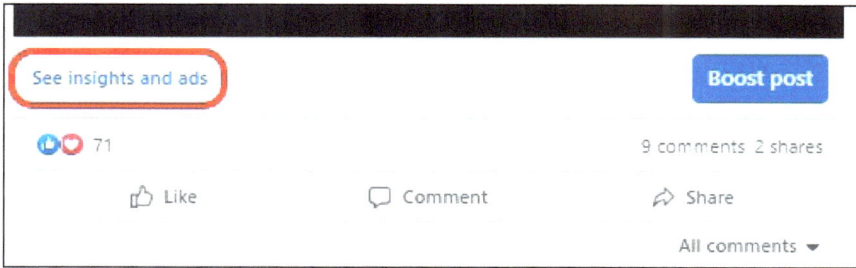

Click this link and screenshot and catalogue the insights statistics pop-up as follows. This will provide critical publication data on:

- Impressions: The number of times your post was on screen.
- Reach: The number of people who saw any of your posts at least once. Reach is different from impressions, which may include multiple views of your posts by the same people. This metric is estimated.
- Engagement: The number of times people engaged with your post through reactions, comments, shares, views and clicks.

Save this screenshot image in the appropriate page folder using the same naming convention as the folder and the thread details, and append with *insights*. For example:

- EnjoyDarkChocolateBusinessPage-MyHappyWorldChocolateDayPost-20201007-insights

SCREENSHOTTING INDIVIDUAL COMMENTS

Following the same approach as for the full threads, adjust the size and position of your browser window to include the URL, and the date and time, and then take screenshots of the individual defamatory posts, comments or reviews, as well as any sub-comments.

Save each screenshot image in the individual offender's folder and title each image with the same naming convention as the full thread, plus an appended offender's name and offending-comment number. For example:

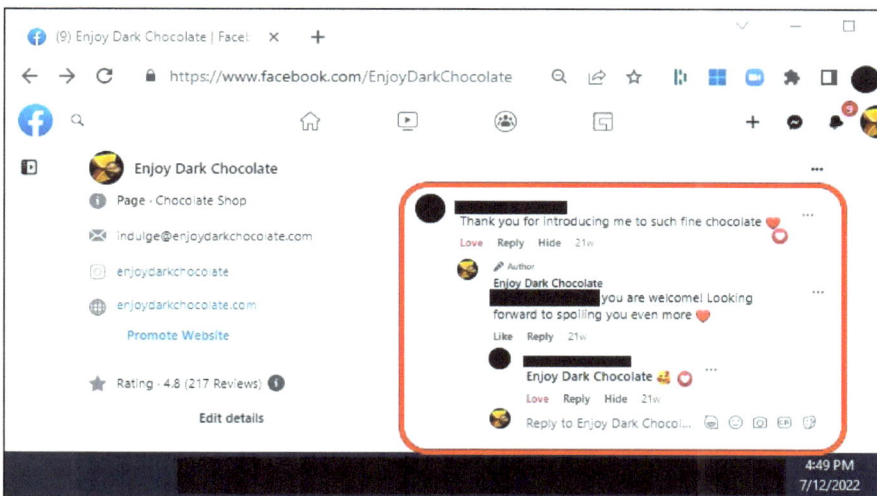

- EnjoyDarkChocolateBusinessPage-MyHappyWorldChocolateDayPost-20201007-MarySmith-Comment1

SCREENSHOTTING EMOJI CLUSTERS

To further support your case, it's important to capture any associated emoji clusters with the defamatory post, comment or review, including any sub-comments. These can serve as additional evidence of publication. To capture them, click on the emoji symbols at the bottom of the review or comment. A pop-up window will appear, showing the profiles of all those who left an emoji. Click on All and then take screenshots of every profile listed. Ensure you capture all contributors by taking as many screenshots as necessary.

Save each screenshot image in the corresponding individual offender's folder, and name each image using the same convention as for the full-thread screenshots, followed by the offender's name and the emoji image number. For example:

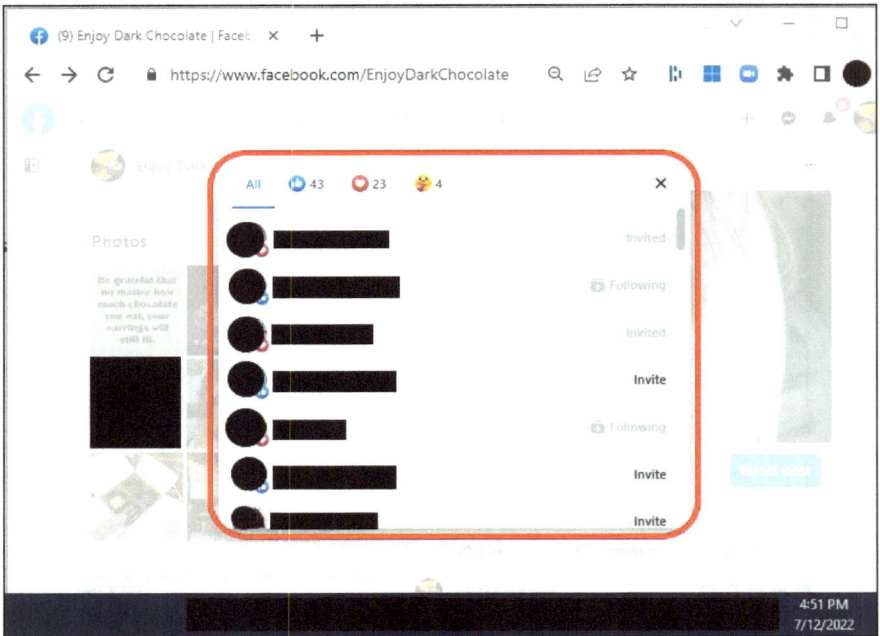

- EnjoyDarkChocolateBusinessPage-MyHappyWorldChocolateDayPost-20201007-MarySmith-Emoji1

SCREENSHOTTING OFFENDING PROFILES

Apply the same process as above for each offender. Click on their profile, then on the About tab, and screenshot the main banner section along with each of the About sub-pages. This will provide valuable information about the offender and help you build a case against them. Make sure to save each screenshot image in the offender's folder, and title them with a clear and concise naming convention. For example:

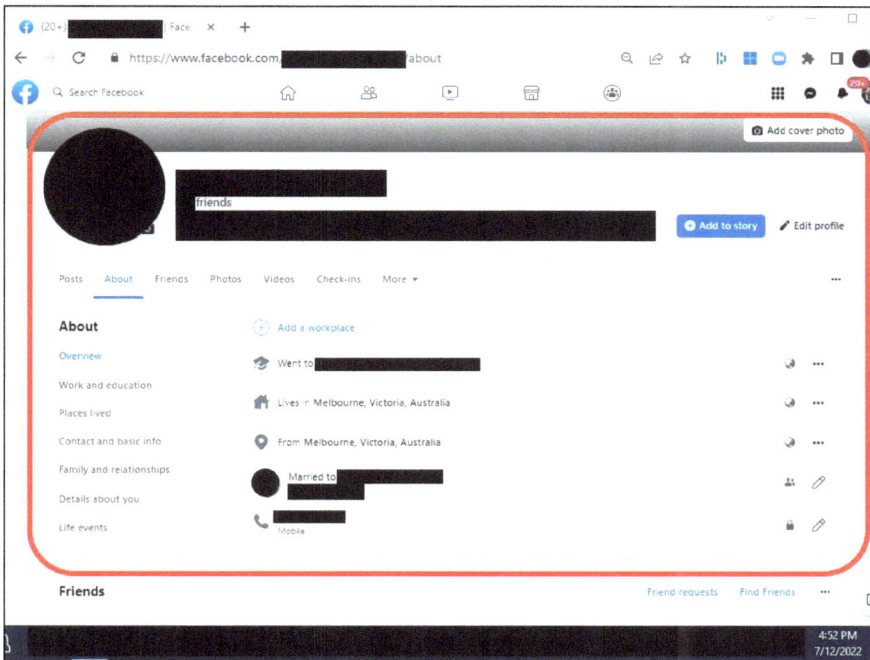

- MarySmith-Profile20201007-Overview

If possible, check the offender's Facebook profile for any other trolling or inflammatory posts or comments they have made against other users, even if the posts are on completely different topics than yours. If you find any such posts, take screenshots of them as well.

STEP 4. REPORT TO FACEBOOK

Despite my own frustration with the lack of assistance I received, as detailed in the chapter **The Help That Never Came**, immediately following the steps above you should report all offensive posts, comments or reviews to Facebook directly. At the time of publishing this guide, Facebook offers the following reporting mechanisms, but this may vary over time and from country to country, so check online for the latest advice and guidance from Facebook and other forums.

- General reporting: https://www.facebook.com/help/reportlinks
- Defamation: https://www.facebook.com/help/contact/430253071144967

As with the steps above, it is important to thoroughly screenshot and catalogue all reports to Facebook before sending them, along with any responses received from Facebook, as proof of your efforts to minimise harm and hopefully restore your reputation and ratings. Save each screenshot image in the individual offender's folder, title each image with the publication details, offender's name, and state whether it's a Facebook report or response. For example:

- EnjoyDarkChocolateBusinessPage-MyHappyWorldChocolateDayPost-20201007-MarySmith-Comment1-FacebookReport

STEP 5. DEMAND REMOVAL AND APOLOGY

Prior to undertaking the following actions, **you should seek immediate and professional legal advice, which may contradict these steps**.

Immediately after completing all the screenshotting above, you should publish a demand to the offenders to remove their publications. To do this, temporarily unblock the offending profiles on your personal or business pages and post a demand similar to the following. Unblocking their profiles is only temporary while you publish your demand and wait for a response.

SUGGESTED DEMAND TEXT

'Your [post, comment, review] above is untrue, offensive and defamatory, and I demand that you remove it immediately. I have already reported it to Facebook and reserve all my rights to take further legal action.'

Again, screenshot the demand and save it in the **individual offender's folder**, and title the image with the same naming convention as the **individual publication,** plus *RemovalDemand*. For example:

• EnjoyDarkChocolateBusinessPage-MyHappyWorldChocolateDayPost-20201007-MarySmith-Comment1-RemovalDemand

Realising that such a demand may well stir the offenders into more attacks, check for responses regularly over the next few days. Depending on their reaction, follow the steps below, **ensuring you capture the date and time in all screenshot images**.

OFFENDER RESPONDS

Should the offenders respond by further commenting, re-block their profile regardless of what they say or do, and again screenshot the entire offending publication, saving each screenshot image in the **individual offender's folder** with the same naming convention as the **individual publication,** plus *RemovalDemandReply*. For example:

- EnjoyDarkChocolateBusinessPage-MyHappyWorldChocolateDayPost-20201007-MarySmith-Comment1-RemovalDemandReply

OFFENDER REMOVES PUBLICATION

If the offender removes their publication, **re-block their profile** (if they haven't done so themselves) and again screenshot the **entire thread section** where the publication appeared previously. Save each screenshot image in in the **individual offender's folder** with the same naming convention as the **individual publication,** plus *[Publication]-Removed,* and note the date and time you first noted the publication removed. For example:

- EnjoyDarkChocolateBusinessPage-MyHappyWorldChocolateDayPost-20201007-MarySmith-Comment1-Removed

OFFENDER DOESN'T RESPOND

If the offender doesn't respond after a day or so, re-block their profile and again screenshot the entire offending publication, saving each screenshot image in the individual offender's folder with the same naming convention as the individual publication, plus *RemovalDemandIgnored*. For example:

- EnjoyDarkChocolateBusinessPage-
  MyHappyWorldChocolateDayPost-20201007-MarySmith-Comment1-
  RemovalDemandIgnored

Well done. You now have lots of evidence to support future legal action, if
that is what you choose to do. You should now hide all offending publications,
where possible. You may also delete the offenders' profiles from your friends
or followers, if that provides greater peace of mind; however, I recommend
leaving them blocked as this provides more options going forward.

OTHER ACTIONS

THE AUTHORITIES

You may also want to report the attack and attackers to the police and or any
online-safety regulators that have authority within your country or jurisdiction.
However, as I explained in the chapter **The Help That Never Came**, my
experience is that these authorities are still a long way from properly protecting
all of us from online harm, so be prepared for some potential frustration.

REMAINING PUBLICATION

You should also take periodic—say, monthly—screenshots of any offending
publications that remain online beyond your control, such as reviews. As
painful as it is to return to these over and over again, this will help prove
the length and reach of the publications. In particular, should you choose to
pursue legal action, **screenshot any remaining publications immediately
prior to sending your first legal demands to the offenders**. My experience
was that most offenders removed their posts immediately after receiving the
first legal demands, which meant that doing another round of screenshots
just prior really helped my legal case.

DON'T REPUBLISH

As I discussed in the chapter titled **The Help That Never Came,** I made the mistake of republishing some of the defamatory comments as part of a post to my friends and clients in an attempt to explain the attacks and minimise harm. However, this republishing was alleged to have contributed to the publication of the original posts and to my own harm, which ultimately minimised the culpability of the offenders. If you feel compelled to share what's happening to you, simply describe the attack without referencing, copying or linking to the publications directly, similar to what I have done throughout this book.

APPENDIX II. BACKGROUND TO THE FORMER CONFLICT BETWEEN ARMENIA AND AZERBAIJAN

Numerous online resources, including those mentioned at the end of this appendix, explain in detail the origins, intricacies, and current state of the conflict between Armenia and Azerbaijan. Thus, the following summary serves only to contextualise my attackers' motivations and not as an in-depth analysis or commentary.

At the end of 1987, Armenia, in addition to the forceful expulsion of hundreds of thousands of Azerbaijanis from their homes in Armenia, launched groundless territorial claims to an inalienable part of Azerbaijan – the Karabakh region.[7] At the time, the Union of the Soviet Socialist Republics still existed.

However, in the early 1990s, when the Soviet Union was falling apart and the soviet republics, including Armenia and Azerbaijan, were one by one proclaiming their independence, Armenia unleashed a devastating war against Azerbaijan. As a result, a significant part of Azerbaijan, including the Karabakh region, was occupied. This military occupation lasted almost for 30 years.

The war claimed the lives of thousands of innocent Azerbaijanis and even more were injured. The largest massacre against civilians was committed in Khojaly, a town occupied by the armed forces of Armenia on February 26, 1992. Over just one night, 613 Azerbaijanis, including 106 women and 63

---

7   The name "Karabakh" comes from the word "Qarabağ" (Garabagh) in the Azerbaijani language. The word Qarabağ (Garabagh) constitutes a compound of two Azerbaijani words: "qara" (black or dense) and "bağ" (garden or forest).

children, were killed and the town itself was totally destroyed. Also, 1,275 Khojaly residents were taken hostage. To this day, 150 people from Khojaly remain missing.

The national legislative bodies of 18 countries, as well as 24 states of the USA, the Organization of Islamic Cooperation and the Organization of Turkic States have adopted several resolutions and decisions condemning the massacre of civilians in Khojaly and have characterised it as a crime against humanity and an act of genocide.

In its judgement of 22 April 2010, the European Court on Human Rights arrived at an important conclusion concerning the crimes committed in Khojaly, denouncing the behaviour of those carrying out the atrocities as "acts of particular gravity which may amount to war crimes or crimes against humanity". In general, 3890 citizens of Azerbaijan, including 71 children, 267 women, and 326 elderly, are still missing as a result of the conflict and their fate is still unknown.

Also, more than 800,000 Azerbaijanis became internally displaced people as a result of the conflict. Additionally, as it was mentioned above, about 250,000 Azerbaijanis were expelled from their homes in Armenia at the end of the 1980s and thus the number of Azerbaijani refugees and internally displaced persons exceeded one million.

So many beautiful cities, including my lovely Shusha, a cultural capital of Azerbaijan, as well as other cities, towns and villages were destroyed and plundered during the years of the military occupation.

The international community rejected the attempts of Armenia to annex the territories of Azerbaijan. International organisations, including the United Nations, Non-Aligned Movement, OIC, NATO, Council of Europe, European Parliament and others, adopted numerous documents in this regard. For instance, the United Nations Security Council in its Resolutions 822 (1993), 853 (1993), 874 (1993), and 884 (1993):

- Confirmed Karabakh and other territories occupied by Armenia as integral parts of the Republic of Azerbaijan

- Condemned the use of force against Azerbaijan and the occupation of its territories, and reaffirmed respect for the sovereignty and territorial integrity of Azerbaijan, the inviolability of international borders, and the inadmissibility of the use of force for the acquisition of territory

- Demanded the immediate, complete and unconditional withdrawal of all Armenian forces from all occupied territories of the Republic of Azerbaijan.

The positions of other international organisations were in line with the above-mentioned resolutions of the UN Security Council.

For the duration of the conflict, Azerbaijan repeatedly stated that the settlement of the conflict was possible only based on the norms and principles of international law, i.e., that with full respect for the sovereignty and territorial integrity of the Republic of Azerbaijan within its state borders, Armenia should withdraw its armed forces from all occupied territories of Azerbaijan, and the right of the forcibly displaced population to return to their homes should be ensured.

Despite decades of diplomatic efforts, facilitated by international mediators – the OSCE Minsk Group Co-Chairs, comprising the Russian Federation, France, and the United States of America – the conflict remained unresolved.

Moreover, despite a ceasefire established in 1994, the armed forces of Armenia regularly violated it and escalated the situation at the frontline by targeting the Azerbaijani civilians residing on the other side of the line of occupation. The leadership of this country presented the occupation of the Azerbaijani territories and the expulsion of the population from these areas as a "gorgeous victory" and glorified those who committed atrocities against the peaceful Azerbaijani population.

From July 2020, Armenian armed provocations escalated. In late September 2020, in response to yet another armed attack by the armed forces of Armenia, Azerbaijan exercised its inherent right of self-defence and undertook a counter-offensive operation to protect its civilian population. This operation lasted for 44 days and became known as the 44-Day War. In the course of these hostilities, many cities, towns and villages in Azerbaijan, including several located far from the conflict zone, came under heavy Armenian shelling. As a result, around 100 Azerbaijani civilians, including children, were killed, and more than 450 were wounded.

Despite this, the counter-offensive operation resulted in the liberation of a large part of the occupied territories of Azerbaijan. It ended on November 10, 2020, through the signing of the trilateral Statement by the President of Azerbaijan, the Prime Minister of Armenia, and the President of the Russian Federation. Under this agreement, Armenia had to withdraw from remaining Azerbaijani-occupied territories, in parallel to the deployment of the Russian peacekeeping contingent for 5 years. As such, it put an end to the almost three-decade-long illegal occupation by Armenia.

The end of the conflict could have marked the beginning of peace and stability in the region. Unfortunately, Armenia continued to violate its commitments under the November 10th Trilateral Statement by refusing to fully withdraw its armed formations from the territories of Azerbaijan where the Russian peacekeeping contingent was temporarily deployed. It further continued military build-up and also installed landmines in the territories of Azerbaijan, causing casualties among Azerbaijanis, including civilians.

Continued military and other provocations by Armenia, and the subordinate regime it had established in the territory of Azerbaijan, forced Azerbaijan to launch localised counter-terror measures in September 2023. As a result, in less than 24 hours Armenian armed formations agreed to fully withdraw from Azerbaijan and dissolve the illegal regime. Finally, the rule of law and public order across all the conflict-affected areas of Azerbaijan was restored.

REFERENCE MATERIAL

Contested Territories and International Law: A Comparative Study of the
Nagorno-Karabakh Conflict and the Aland Islands Precedent
Author: Kamal Makili-Aliyev, Associate Professor of Human Rights

To read: https://www.taylorfrancis.com/books/
oa-mono/10.4324/9780429353437/contested-territories-internation-
al-law-kamal-makili-aliyev?fbclid=IwAR1SA7HoUow1JVShGv7dsar-
gAx3yoqM4zr2Bu674W9UC380yOJ24ddljWwQ

To buy the book: https://www.routledge.com/Contested-Territories-
and-International-Law-A-Comparative-Study-of-the/Makili-Aliyev/p/
book/9780367373825?fbclid=IwAR2UXtNgnn93AlB8OXyliH1Wud-
3jBQtpJV6FbsZR4yE9m3L7eyGKP8GylK4#

This book considers the possibilities for resolution of the Nagorno-Karabakh Conflict in the context of comparative international law. The armed conflict between Armenia and Azerbaijan over the territory of the Nagorno-Karabakh has been on the peace and security agenda since the dissolution of the Soviet Union. This volume draws parallels with a similar situation between Sweden and Finland over the sovereignty of the Aland Islands in the early 20th century. Resolved in 1921, it is argued that this represents a model autonomy solution for territorial conflicts that include questions of territorial integrity, self-determination, and minority rights. The book compares both conflict situations from the international law perspective, finding both commonalities and dissimilarities. It advances the application of the solution found in the Aland Islands precedent as a model for the resolution of the Nagorno-Karabakh Conflict, and provides appropriate recommendations for its implementation. The book will be of interest to academics, researchers, and policymakers in the areas of international law and security, conflict resolution, and international relations.

Azerbaijan Diary: A Rogue Reporter's Adventures in an Oil-rich, War-torn, Post-Soviet Republic - 1st Edition
Author: Thomas Goltz

https://www.amazon.com/Azerbaijan-Diary-Reporters-Adventures-Post-Soviet/dp/076560244X

This underground classic tells the story of oil-rich Azerbaijan's first years of independence from Moscow. Goltz's vivid, personal account, filled with memorable portraits of individuals in high places and low, carries the reader from the battlefront to the oilfield, the voting booth to the negotiating table, always with an astute sense of how it all fits into the geopolitical firmament.

In its first years as an independent state, the former Soviet republic of Azerbaijan was a prime example of post-Soviet chaos—beset by coups and civil strife, and losing the Karabakh war of secession, with a fifth of its territory occupied by Armenian troops. Azerbaijan may be endowed with vast oil reserves, but it also bestrides one of the greatest ethnic, religious, and political faultlines in the world.

Thomas Goltz became an accidental witness to Azerbaijan's inglorious history-in-the- making when he was detoured into Baku in mid-1991 -- and decided to stay. This record of his years there alternates in style between tragedy and farce. Throughout, the intensity of immediate experience is balanced by an acute awareness of contemporaneous events in Karabakh and Nakhjivan, Georgia and Armenia, Russia and Chechnya, Iran and Turkey, Washington and Houston.

The Endless Corridor
An award-winning documentary. Directors: Aleksandras Brokas, Mindaugas Urbonavicius

https://www.youtube.com/watch?v=pG7YsHpUw1w

Narrated by Jeremy Irons, this definitive account tells of the heart-wrenching human rights tragedy in 1992 when hundreds of Azerbaijanis were massacred after Armenians stormed the city of Khojaly. The film includes interviews with survivors, eyewitnesses and journalists who covered the events, as well as rare footage and photos from the time of the tragedy.

Karabakh in 44 Days: From Occupation to Liberation
Author: Irish historian, Dr. Patrick Walsh

APPENDIX III. THE 2022 NATIONAL ONLINE SAFETY SURVEY

The following statistics from the Australian eSafety Commissioner are some of the most important I have seen on the issue of online harm. However, these are only a small subset relating to cyberbullying, therefore I encourage everyone to download, read, and share this **free** report:

https://www.infrastructure.gov.au/sites/default/files/documents/national-online-safety-survey-2022-wcag-accessible-report-25july2022-final.pdf

6.4.1. EXPERIENCES OF ONLINE HARM (INCIDENCE AND FREQUENCY IN LAST 12 MONTHS)

More than one-third of Australian adults (net 39.93%) indicate that they have experienced at least one of the negative online behaviours prompted for in the survey in the last 12 months (refer Table 27). More than one-fifth (20.74%) report being sent or coming across unwanted or inappropriate sexual content online, and 12.93% report receiving repeated unwanted contact by someone who was not a business or organisation.

TABLE 27: NEGATIVE ONLINE EXPERIENCES IN THE LAST 12 MONTHS (% ADULTS)

Behaviour experienced	%
I was sent, or came across, unwanted or inappropriate sexual content online	20.74
I received repeated unwanted online contact by someone who was not a business or organisation	12.93
I was sent, or came across, unwanted or inappropriate violent content online	9.68
Someone pretended to be me online	7.08
Someone electronically tracked my location or monitored or movements without my permission	5.93
I was called offensive names online	5.47
I was ridiculed or made fun of online	4.81
I received online communication that offended, denigrated or abused me because of my identity or beliefs	4.60
I was sent, or came across, online content that promoted or provided instructions for drug use	4.10
I was sent, or came across, online content that promoted or provided instructions in self-harm	3.78
Lies or rumours were spread about me online	2.85
I was threatened by someone who said they would send or post private photos or videos of me (nude or semi-nude or sexual) without my permission	2.74
Someone threatened to harm or abuse me	2.68
Private photos or videos of me (nude or semi-nude or sexual) were shared online or electronically without my permission	1.17

6.5.1. SUMMARY: PERPETRATORS AND USE OF ALIASES

Exploration of the use of aliases by perpetrators was a new area of enquiry in the 2022 National Online Safety Survey.

A minority of adults (net 5.50%) have perpetrated online harm towards someone else, with 2.39% acknowledging that they have either ridiculed or made fun of someone, and 1.84% that they have called someone offensive names online. This low rate of perpetrators is in contrast, however, to the 39.93% who indicated that they had been on the receiving end of online harm.

The identity of the perpetrator(s) was mostly unknown to the target of the negative online experience, and this was the case regardless of whether there was one person responsible (64.31%), or multiple or an unknown number of people responsible (56.63%).

Over half of all adults (54.31%) report that they used their real name or account when they carried out these activities, however, 25.82% did it anonymously, and 18.11% used a fake or made-up name.

For intent behind the negative online actions, 37.30% report that they meant it as a joke.

CONTACT ME

WEBSITE

www.KhuramanArmstrong.com

*Includes Enjoy Dark Chocolate page, AgelessYou pages,
Culture and Cuisine page, and Contact Me form.*

FACEBOOK

/KhuramanArmstrong

INSTAGRAM

/KhuramanArmstrong

LINKEDIN

/khuramanarmstrong

www.ingramcontent.com/pod-product-compliance
Lightning Source LLC
Chambersburg PA
CBHW040929030426
42334CB00002B/14